IN EVERY KID THERE LURKS A TIGER

IN EVERY KID THERE LURKS A TIGER

Rudy Duran's five-step programme
to teach you and your child the
fundamentals of golf

Rudy Duran with Rick Lipsey

To Bud and Joyce Lorbeer
Thank you for your support over the last thirty years.
Without it, none of my success would have been possible.
– Rudy

This edition first published in Great Britain in 2002 by
Virgin Books Ltd
Thames Wharf Studios
Rainville Road
London W6 9HA

First published in the United States of America in 2002 by Hyperion

Published by arrangement with Hyperion,
an imprint of Buena Vista Books Inc.

A catalogue record for the book is available from the British Library.

ISBN 0 7535 0701 3

Typeset by TW Typesetting, Plymouth, Devon
Printed and bound in Great Britain by
Mackays of Chatham PLC

CONTENTS

We are all capable of more than we do.
— MARY BAKER EDDY

INTRODUCTION

I didn't know Rudy Duran from Duran Duran when my phone rang on a dank afternoon in January 2000. I was sitting in my eighteenth-floor office in the Time and Life Building in New York, looking down at Radio City Music Hall. On the other end of the line was my fellow *Sports Illustrated* golf writer, Jaime Diaz, calling from his home in Temecula, California. 'Rick, I've got a great story idea,' Jaime said. 'It's about Rudy Duran. Rudy was Tiger's first childhood golf coach, and the PGA Tour just gave him the Card Walker Award.'

It doesn't take much to sell a story about Tiger to *SI*'s editors. So when I told one of them about Rudy, his experience with Tiger and the Card Walker award – given annually by the Tour for contributions to junior golf – I got an instantaneous go-ahead to do a piece with Rudy.

A minute later I had Rudy on the line and was feverishly typing. Rudy's tales were vivid, providing fresh insight into how Tiger became such a great golfer, and I felt like I'd discovered the Dead Sea Scrolls. Rudy spoke about his years teaching Tiger (from age four to ten), his close friendship with Tiger's parents, Earl and Tida, and his own inspiring career as one of the country's premier teachers. Rudy also recounted his days as a fledgling tour pro, cutting his teeth on mini tours in Canada and the United States. He talked about his involvement with the PGA of America's Southern California Section, the First Tee national junior golf initiative, the National Minority Golf Foundation and many other not-for-profit golf organisations.

I felt humbled and, to be honest, a little ignorant. Here was one of the game's most influential teachers, but I had never heard of him. How was that possible? Hadn't every nook and cranny of Tiger's life already been exploited?

Apparently not, and Rudy liked it that way. He could have easily cashed in on his intimate relationship with the Woodses, but Rudy is not interested in fame. He prefers peace and quiet, friendships and laughs – and, of course, having fun on the golf course regardless of the score. Indeed, Rudy downplays his immense contribution to Tiger's development as a person and as a golfer. 'Tiger was an uncut diamond who needed a little shaping and grinding,' says Rudy. 'I just happened to be the person who provided the first cuts.'

So it came as no surprise that when I asked Rudy if he wanted to write this book, he was dead set against it. 'Why would I want to write a book?' Rudy said in his California twang. 'I've got everything I need and more lessons than I can handle.'

It took every ounce of my persuasion powers to convince Rudy to do the book. He didn't perk up when I explained to him that his five-step programme for learning golf was pure genius, and that it could benefit lifelong as well as aspiring golfers around the world. Nor did Rudy seem excited about the chance to get his name into the permanent record of the Library of Congress. I think I finally hooked Rudy by telling him that he wouldn't have to type a word, that all he had to do was talk. 'Okay, Rick,' he said. 'I like that, because I *love* to talk.'

Rudy also loves to eat. I learned that during the three week-long trips I made to Rudy's house in San Luis Obispo, California, last year. Barbecue, Chinese, Italian, Mexican, Thai – Rudy loves every food known to man, including artichokes. Funny, though, I had just two home-cooked meals during three weeks at Rudy's home. See, Rudy's kitchen is perhaps the most unused kitchen in California. One morning, I thought about planning a spaghetti dinner, but I quashed the idea after looking through his cabinets and discovering that he didn't own a pot big enough to boil spaghetti.

Despite Rudy's aversion to cooking, he is as big-hearted a host as I've ever met. Rudy not only opened up his house, giving me an entire floor, but he also let me borrow his minivan to go wherever I wanted, and he put me in charge of the remote control to his TV. 'My only caveat is that you mute all golf telecasts,' Rudy said. As you might expect, Rudy enjoys watching golf tournaments on TV, but he doesn't like the exaggerated commentary, so for years he's been muting the sound while watching.

Time flew during the days and nights at Rudy's. We spent most of the time in his living room. I sat at one end of a new cherry-wood table and Rudy was at the other end. Our only distractions were the occasional call on Rudy's cellphone and the *baaa-haaa, baaa-haaa* sounds echoing from the sheep that graze in his neighbour's yard.

I learned a lot about Rudy during our time together, and I feel as if we developed a genuine friendship. Some of the titbits I picked up about him include his favourite words ('skosh' and 'dude'); that he, like I, is a hunt-and-peck typist; that his penchant for speed (he used to drive Porsches) has been replaced by an appreciation for relaxation (he now drives a Ford Windstar minivan); and that he was never paid anything for teaching Tiger or some of the other kids who have been his pupils. That last fact astonished me, but there's a good explanation.

The son of an automobile upholsterer and a housewife, Rudy didn't have access to golf as a kid. He didn't take up the game in earnest until the year after he graduated from high school, in 1968, and joined the US Air Force. Rudy played almost every day during his military duty, competing on the base teams at the various places at which he was stationed throughout Europe and the United States. After being honourably discharged from the Air Force early in 1971, Rudy turned pro at the end of the year. His goal was to play on the PGA Tour, but knowing that making the Tour was a long shot, he also pursued work as a club pro to assure himself a steady pay cheque.

For most of the 1970s, Rudy split his time between teaching and playing. By 1978, Rudy was still in mini-tour purgatory, and he had the good sense to shelve his tour aspirations and devote himself to teaching. As soon as Rudy began teaching, he made a personal vow to dedicate a portion of his time to kids, giving them lessons at little or no cost. Rudy wanted to provide kids with something that he had never had as a child: easy access to the game and an organised junior programme. 'I teach kids because I love it,' says Rudy, now in his mid-fifties. 'Plus, I learn as much from them as they do from me.'

I got a glimpse into Rudy's teaching genius by watching him give lessons. Rudy works at two public courses in central California, Chalk Mountain, in Atascadero, and the Links at Paso Robles, in Paso Robles. Rudy has owned the master lease to Chalk since he moved to San Luis Obispo from Long Beach in 1981. However, he continued teaching Tiger until 1986, making four-hour drives south on Highway 101 to work with his prized pupil. When Rudy couldn't continue to make the journey with enough regularity, Earl took Tiger to another top-notch instructor, John Anselmo, who would teach Tiger for seven years, until Tiger started working with Butch Harmon, his current instructor. Rudy personally built and designed his other course, the Links, and opened it in 1996.

I watched Rudy give lessons to players old and young, male and female, beginner and expert. One lesson stands out. On a crisp Saturday morning at Chalk Mountain, a freshman at Paso Robles High came to Rudy for the first lesson of his life. The boy was with his father, who introduced his son to Rudy. 'Great to meet you,' Rudy said, extending his right hand to greet the boy. The boy's nervousness instantly melted away and was replaced by a wide smile.

Rudy doesn't waste time on the lesson tee, and he talks while his pupils hit shots. On this day, Rudy teed up a few balls in a row and the boy started swinging. As the boy swung, he told Rudy about his golf history. The boy had played golf casually for a couple of years. He didn't remember his best score, but he did know that he wanted to step up his commitment to the game and earn a spot on his high school golf team. 'Sounds like a good goal,' Rudy said.

Rudy cleaned the boy's clubs, one by one, peeking up every now and then to watch his new pupil's swing. 'Great,' Rudy would say after the boy hit an ugly cut-fade. 'Looks good.' The shots didn't look good to me, but what did I know?

Rudy shared a few basics with the boy, explaining the necessary slapping (Rudy also calls it 'whapping') motion you need to hit the ball. He also strengthened the boy's grip and told him that he needed to be in perfect balance to hit good shots. Rudy showed the boy the difference between good and bad balance positions by putting him in each position so he could feel them himself.

After fifteen minutes, the sound of the boy's shots had improved from a weak clicking noise to a solid slap, like a hammer rapping into a nail. Soon, using a 6-iron, the boy was belting 140-yard shots with a tight draw. The father, sitting in a chair about 20 feet behind his son, had a glowing smile. In only a few minutes, Rudy had helped the boy progress from hacker to hitter.

After the lesson, the father signed his son up for another session the following weekend. He and his son then went straight to the driving range to practise. 'My first thought was that making the team would be a stretch,' Rudy told me later. 'But after a little while, I changed my mind. The boy *could* really make the team.'

Rudy's genius is his blend of patience, positivity, sharp eyes and the ability to provide just the right amount of information – not too much and not too little. He's also deadly realistic. He worked with the greatest junior golfer in history, so he knows the difference between a tyke with pro potential and one without it. 'If a kid isn't shooting way under personal par, he's shooting too high to play on tour,' Rudy says.

Rudy is blunt with his young charges and their parents, but they often don't listen. 'Some parents have a hard time accepting how enormous an amount of time and energy it takes to earn a college golf scholarship, or a tour card. And even with all the hard work, there are still no guarantees.'

Still, the parents bring their kids to Rudy, and some spend the weekend in San Luis Obispo, either staying at a motel or, more frequently, at Rudy's house. 'The man has a heart of gold,' says John Archibald, who has been driving his son, J.D., from Simi Valley to see Rudy since 1999, when J.D. was nine years old. 'Rudy is a remarkable study in consistency and professionalism. I feel that the real magic occurs when Rudy gets parent and child working together as a team. It increases an already strong bond, and regardless of our talent level, we all end up feeling like Tigers.'

Rick Lipsey
New York, NY
December 2001

1. IF YOU THINK LIKE A KID, YOU'LL PLAY LIKE A PRO

THIS KID IS GOOD!

In the spring of 1980, Tida Woods walked into my pro shop at Heartwell Golf Park in Long Beach, California. Next to her was her tiny four-year-old son. It was the middle of the afternoon and I was standing behind the counter that held sleeves of balls, bags of tees and other golf paraphernalia. I had never met Tida Woods, but she spoke right up. 'My son is very talented, and my husband and I are interested if you could give him some private lessons,' she said.

That wasn't the first time a parent had asked me to give their daughter or son a few golf lessons. I had been running a popular junior golf programme at Heartwell for nearly a decade. But I had never before been asked to work one-on-one with somebody as young as Tiger. *He was a four-year-old, for God's sake!* After hesitating for a moment, I told Tida, 'Let's go to the practice range and have your son hit a few shots.'

The three of us walked to the range, where the boy pulled a sawed-off 21½ wood from his bag. I teed up a few balls and he hit them one after another. He was in perfect balance, and he hit each ball 60 to 70 yards with a nice draw.

Tiger's mannerisms were like those of a very experienced player, yet I knew he couldn't be very experienced, because he was only four. After watching a few more swings, I was convinced that Tiger wasn't a typical junior golfer. It doesn't take long to identify genius.

I told Tida, 'I'd be happy to work with your son, and he can play here any time he wants.'

For the next six years, I worked with the Woods family to provide the best environment in which their son could develop his game. Tiger and I spent many afternoons competing against each other, practising different shots at the range, and talking about golf and life. After playing and practising, Earl, Tiger and I would chat for hours about the game and how much fun it was. We'd have brainstorming sessions either in the clubhouse or at the Woodses' house in Cypress, California.

Without knowing they were doing it, Tiger (and Earl) were teaching me plenty of things about golf, especially about how to teach the game. In the years we worked together, Tiger taught me how to be a better instructor. I learned that kids need personally fitted clubs, just like adults. I created a personal par system for Tiger, and eventually expanded the system to include golfers of all levels. Tiger was unquestionably my most skilled student, but not everything about him was unique. Most young people play golf with a lot of confidence and rarely get depressed over bad shots.

Thinking positively is, in fact, the most overlooked skill in golf. Beginners and young players shouldn't worry about technique, especially when they first learn golf. There will be plenty of time to iron out the finer points after they've been playing for a while. The first bit of advice I always give to new students is this: Hit it as far as you can.

In this book, I will give young golfers the tools they need to learn and play golf at the highest level their dreams and abilities can take them.

Playing the best golf you can is achieved by learning the game's fundamentals – swing technique and general knowledge – and then utilising that information, along with your own unique style, to shoot as low as you can. Sounds almost too easy, doesn't it? It's not.

My five-step programme is geared specifically for beginners and young golfers, and you don't need any prior golf experience. You do, however, need a deep desire to learn about golf and have fun.

The programme is organised into four disciplines – Putting, Less-than-Full Swing, Full Swing and General Knowledge – and each discipline is divided into five separate levels. Golfers progress through the programme, from level to level, at their own pace. Some golfers will complete the entire curriculum in a few months; for others it may take a few years. The time, though, doesn't matter. What's important is to complete the programme at a pace that's comfortable for *you*.

Becoming a competent golfer doesn't require you to master mountains of technical knowledge or to develop a 'perfect swing'. Nobody knows everything about the swing, and nobody ever has, or ever will, possess a perfect swing. Your golf swing is like your handwriting – it's individual and unique. There are ways to improve your swing just as there are ways to improve your handwriting. But rather than adopting a completely new style or radical technique, you are almost always better off refining and perfecting your own style and learning to use your style more often.

If I gave most golfers – even beginners – ten chances to hit a good drive on the first tee, they would probably hit at least one decent shot. I believe everyone has the ability to hit a golf ball well. My goal is to help you learn to utilise your good swing more frequently.

WHAT GOLF IS ALL ABOUT

1. Virtually everybody has the ability to play golf decently. I've seen blind people and people with one leg play golf well. I've seen people in wheelchairs hit 200-yard shots. Golf isn't a matter of *if* you can play well. It's a question of if you *want* to play well.
2. Golf is about using and improving your skills, savouring the joys, trials and tribulations that every player experiences on and off the course, the good lies and the bad lies.
3. Golf is about pulling off impossible shots, spending a few hours with family and friends and enjoying beautiful scenery. Ask any avid golfer to rattle off his favourite memories and you won't hear much about scores. That's because golf isn't about the score.
4. Golf is about hitting the ball as well as you can from different locations, in different conditions and with different clubs. If you're playing golf for perfection, or if you're trying to make

a certain score, you probably shouldn't be playing, because it's unlikely that you'll ever be happy on the course.

5. Golf is about consistency. The one similarity from shot to shot, and round to round, is your swing. You use one basic swing motion, varying only its size and power, to hit virtually all golf shots, even putts.

Ben Hogan was one of the best golfers in history. He won 63 PGA Tour events – the third highest total ever – and in 1953 he won all three major championships he entered: the Masters, US Open and British Open. Hogan didn't enter the PGA Championship because it was held so close to the British that he couldn't get from Carnoustie, Scotland, to Birmingham, Michigan, in time for the tournament.

Hogan also understood the golf swing better than most people did, and he believed that anyone, with a fair amount of effort and practice, could learn to play golf well. In his classic book *The Modern Fundamentals of Golf*, Hogan writes,

> *Up to a considerable point, as I see it, there's nothing difficult about golf, nothing. I see no reason, truly, why the average golfer, if he goes about it intelligently, shouldn't play in the 70s – and I mean by playing the type of shots a fine golfer plays.*

If you keep my five truths in mind, and if you remember the wise advice of Ben Hogan, you're always going to have fun, and you're always going to play good – maybe even great – golf.

SETTING GOALS

In golf – as in life – it's important to keep track of your goals. If the LPGA or PGA Tour is your ultimate goal, you may need to know more than my programme can teach you. But you might not. Fred Couples is one of the many professional players who have made it to the Tour with hardly any personal instruction. Whatever your goals may be, whether they are to make the Tour, to play in your school or college team, or to simply play with friends, you'll need to develop what many instructors call 'golf's intangibles.' These include faith in your swing, an open mind, and feel and imagination on the course.

There's no formula for learning golf's intangibles. They are skills that you absorb more than learn. The only way to develop these intangibles is to expose yourself to all facets of the game – through playing and practice, talking about golf, watching the game on TV, reading about it and just hanging around the course and other golfers.

The intangibles are what separate top-notch golfers from the rest of the pack. Most of the time, intangibles determine your success rate. That's the rate at which you hit good shots. Professional golfers hit good shots most of the time, but certainly not all of the time. Most casual golfers think they rarely, if ever, hit good shots. That's not true.

Here's a fact that might startle you: many amateurs could play on the PGA Tour – if they were given multiple chances to hit every shot. Try it yourself. Play a round hitting two shots from every position, and then select the best shot of the pair. You'll be shocked at how low you can shoot. Most golfers are more skilled than they think they are. The goal, then, should be to learn how to execute the good swing more frequently, rather than developing a new swing.

THINK POSITIVE, THINK LIKE A KID

Before you begin my programme, I want you to do something most golfers never learn to do. I want you to erase virtually everything you've heard about how hard golf is. Zap those thoughts. If you're going to be as good as you can be, and have fun, you've got to delete negative ideas that will limit your enjoyment of the game.

Golf is impossible? *Ignore it!* Long bunker shots are the hardest shots in golf? Forget it! Left-to-right putts are harder than right-to-left putts, for right-handed players? Don't believe it for a second! That type of pessimistic – and totally untrue – thinking is one of the biggest roadblocks to playing good golf.

To play well, you've got to think like a kid. If you are a kid and you want to play well, be yourself. Keep your mind free of prejudice, fear and doubt. What's the worst thing that could happen on the golf course? You hit a ball into the water? Big deal. Who knows? Your ball might land on the edge of the water, and then you'll have a chance to hit a magnificent recovery shot.

Each time you address the ball, expect the best to happen, and keep your thoughts unbiased, uninhibited and untainted by other people's expectations. Come to the practice tee full of hope. The past has no influence on the present, unless you let it.

I've spent many days playing golf with Tiger, beginning when he was four years old, but I can't recall him ever saying that golf is a difficult game. To Tiger, everything about golf is exciting and fun. Every shot represents an opportunity to do something extraordinary, to discover a more effective way of hitting the ball in different situations or to create a new method of hitting a routine shot. Even after he'd been taking lessons from me for a few years, Tiger didn't think too much about his swing. His sole mission was to hit the ball at the target.

TIGER'S PERFECT 10

Tiger and I used to play a few rounds every month. When he was ten, we visited Mesa Verde Country Club in Costa Mesa, California. The tenth hole, a 424-yard par 4, has a lake between the tee and the fairway, and the tee shot requires a 100-yard carry over the lake. From the championship tees, Tiger had to hit a perfect drive to carry the water.

His first drive that day landed in the water. After taking a drop on the edge of the lake, he flailed his third shot to the right, and it bounded into the water that guarded the right side of the fairway. After dropping again, Tiger knocked his fifth shot down the fairway, and his sixth shot missed the green. Finally, he chipped on to the green and three-putted for a 10.

It was a terrible score for Tiger, who at that time was regularly shooting under his personal par, which was 5 on this hole. On the 11th tee, I teased him, saying, 'Ha! The world-famous Tiger Woods just made a ten on the tenth hole at

*age ten.' He laughed along with me, and we played the 11th
hole in perfectly good spirits. He was happy as could be,
bounding down the fairway as if nothing unusual had happened
on the previous hole. He had already forgotten about the 10.*

*Even at a young age, Tiger's composure was astonishing.
Most golfers would have been steaming mad or depressed. Tiger
was neither.*

THE ATTITUDE OF POSSIBILITY

Soon after joining the PGA Tour in 1996, Tiger said he thought
he could win every tournament he entered. Of course, every
reporter, golf fan and tour player said Tiger was crazy and
egotistical.

Even after Tiger won two of the first seven Tour events he
entered in autumn 1996 – and the following spring won the
first Masters in which he played as a pro (by 12 shots with a
record score of 18-under 270) – people still thought Tiger was
crazy for thinking that he could win every time he played. Why?
In part, because Tiger said he had lots of room for improvement. *How can you improve on a 12-shot victory at Augusta?* Easy,
in Tiger's eyes. You could win the US Open by 15 strokes,
which Tiger did at Pebble Beach in June 2000. Suffice it to say,
nobody doubts Tiger any more when he talks about what's
possible in golf.

Tiger has never let anybody else's ideas limit him, and neither
should you. Dream big, and then take whatever steps are
necessary to make your dreams come true. But don't forget to
play golf the way it has to be played: one shot at a time, hitting
each shot as well as you can, with no thought of the future and
no thought of the past. If you whiff three times in a row, forget
it. Rip the fourth shot down the fairway and focus on the fifth
shot as you walk to your ball.

HOW WELL WILL YOU PLAY?

Who knows? You might have the potential to be a better golfer
than Tiger Woods is today. When I used to tell people that I
thought Tiger was the best player I'd ever seen, and that he

might turn out to be better than Bobby Jones and Jack Nicklaus, they thought I was out of my mind.

Today, some people think I'm crazy because I believe there are kids who are as good as, and perhaps better than, Tiger was as a junior. Tiger may be the best player in history, but his game is still not perfect. There's better golf to be played, and Tiger knows it.

How much room for improvement is there? There are approximately 80 million children who are 19 or younger in the United States, but fewer than 4 million of those youngsters play golf. So, in theory, there is one Tiger in every 4 million American kids, so it's possible there are at least 19 other Tigers who have never touched a golf club. If golf in the United States ever becomes as popular as soccer in Brazil or ice hockey in Canada, we're going to see a dramatic rise in the skill level of America's top golfers.

IS GOLF AFFORDABLE?

Most people can afford to play golf. Perhaps you can't afford to join a private country club, and you might not be able to afford greens fees at a public course. But money doesn't have to be a barrier for an aspiring golfer of any age, if the player has a sincere desire to learn the game.

Some of the greatest professional golfers in history had minimal financial resources when they were growing up, but they found inexpensive ways to play the game. Some prodigies caddied or worked in the pro shop at a club. The jobs provided free golf because most clubs grant playing privileges to caddies and the pro shop staff. In extreme cases, aspiring but penniless golfers carved clubs out of wood blocks, and played on makeshift courses using branches as flagsticks and food cans as cups.

José Coceres is one of ten brothers from a poor family in the Chaco province of Argentina. José and his brothers couldn't afford golf equipment, but they wanted to become golf pros. That's why they caddied, and carved their own clubs out of trees. After playing for a decade on the European tour, José fulfilled his lifelong dream in April 2001, by winning his first PGA Tour event, the WorldCom Classic in Hilton Head Island, South Carolina. My family's finances weren't as dire as the Cocereses', but my parents couldn't afford to join a club, so I often practised in our backyard, chipping and putting into soup cans.

You probably don't have to go to such extremes as the Cocereses did, however, because most urban areas have affordable – and sometimes free – junior golf programmes. Also there are several low-cost golf instructional programmes geared to adults throughout the country. If you can't find a programme that's suitable for you or your child, contact the PGA pro at a club in your area and explain your situation. Don't worry if you're not a member at the club. Most golf pros are approachable and welcome queries from the public.

THE 15TH CLUB IN YOUR BAG – THE 'FORGET IT' CLUB

A couple of years ago, I watched a young boy doing skateboard stunts in his driveway. One of the stunts involved jumping off a ramp and spinning around 180 degrees. Before each attempt, the boy would call out to his father, 'Look, I'm gonna do it.' But the youngster couldn't do it, and he crashed at least a dozen times. On the 13th try he nailed the landing perfectly and yelled out a satisfied, 'Yeah!' With a huge smile, he looked over to his father and said, 'See, I can do it.'

Like most kids playing sports, this boy quickly deleted the previous failed attempts from his memory, and the only thing on his mind was the leap at hand. This mindset – having the ability to dwell on the good and delete the bad – comes naturally to young people, and it's a perspective that's essential for golf.

SMILE

Here's a little sociology experiment I'd like you to try. Sit by the first tee at a golf course for half an hour and look at the faces of the golfers. If your course is like mine, you won't see many smiles. Golf is supposed to be fun, but it often doesn't look as if many golfers are having fun. Why? What's the point of spending four hours doing something that barely makes you crack a grin?

The dearth of happy faces is troubling, and several of golf's top teaching experts have taken notice of this trend. Two of them, Lynn Marriott and Pia Nilsson, who work closely with the First Tee programme, say that smiling on the course is not just good for your well-being, it will help lower your scores, too. A golfer with high ability and a bad attitude can play good golf, but that same golfer will play better with a good attitude. The two mindsets that are most conducive to playing good golf are neutral and positive. A negative mindset can be a detriment to playing your best golf.

Smiling won't only benefit you. People who are inclined to smile are more desirable to be around than people who frown. Nobody wants to play golf with a scowler. I know, because I rarely used to smile on the course, and I can't remember a single instance where my lack of smiling served me well. However, I recall many times when it hurt my game – and spoiled my playing partners' experiences too.

Smiles are a big reason Sergio Garcia and Matt Kuchar were immediately popular when they made their tour debuts. Remember Sergio smiling his way through the 1999 PGA Championship at Medinah, where he battled Tiger down to the last hole and lost by a single stroke? Or Matt Kuchar, who rode his infectious grin into the hearts of golf fans around the world in 1998 at the Masters and US Open, two major championships in which he was the low amateur?

Magic Johnson, the basketball star who led the Los Angeles Lakers to five NBA titles in the 1980s, epitomised how effectively a smile can energise spectators and one's own performance. Even when Johnson and his teammates were not playing well, he usually smiled, and his team usually rallied around his positive energy.

PGA Tour player Loren Roberts also has a terrific perspective. Loren says, 'You have to try as hard as you can, but you can't care about the result.' That's Loren's version of a positive attitude. Loren doesn't smile too much on the course, but he never frowns. He stays even-keeled no matter what the situation, and that's a big reason he's been on the Tour for over twenty years. By the end of 2000, Loren was in his mid-forties and playing some of the best golf of his career, having climbed into the top 25 in the World Rankings for the first time.

GOOD GOLF TALK

Golfers love to talk about their rounds after playing. The post-round debriefing is one of the game's great rituals. Foursomes huddle in the clubhouse or snack bar and replay with total recall every highlight and lowlight. Too often, however, people dwell on the lowlights, the 'what ifs'. They recount the shots they almost hit well, or bounces they feel were unfair, and work out what they would have scored had they got a few good breaks.

Such chatter might seem fun, but it can be counterproductive. Listen to interviews with Tiger or any other top professional. They rarely discuss mistakes or blame poor shots or bad holes on anything but themselves. Tiger has a knack for finding a silver lining in almost every round. He knows reviewing the positive events of the round are much more helpful than dwelling on the negative ones.

After your next round, try thinking and talking only about the good things that happened. You'll be surprised how challenging this exercise is, but you'll definitely be pleased with the results.

ADMIT IT – YOU ARE TALENTED

In the late 1980s, I went to a series of seminars that were produced by the Summit Organisation, which was known for helping people from all walks of life improve their attitudes. At one meeting, every attendee was asked to stand in front of the group and say something positive about him- or herself. Everybody stood up and said something, but it wasn't easy.

After the exercise, several people said they had a tough time thinking of something positive to say. I was shocked – everybody's got a lot of good qualities, but I hadn't realised how bashful people are about openly sharing their positive talents and qualities.

Golfers need to be confident in their abilities and feel free to express those abilities without feeling conceited.

A woman in her early thirties who had been seriously playing golf for 16 months once came to me for a lesson. She was still topping one of every three or four shots, but her good swings produced expert-level results. This woman was especially good at chipping and hitting mid-irons. However, when I asked her what was the best part of her game, she said there was no best part.

'I'm not good at anything,' she said. That wasn't true, of course, but to her it was true, and not admitting that she had talent was a big reason she rarely played up to her potential. She and I talked about the need for her to open up and admit that she was a talented golfer. Once she did that, she began talking more positively about her game, and her scores began improving.

Positive talk doesn't just pertain to discussions after a round or on the practice tee. It's also important to be upbeat while you're on the course. If there's a lake between your ball and the hole, don't think, 'I'm going to play safe and hit to the left to avoid the water.' Instead, focus on what you must do to hit a good shot: 'I'm going to make a big turn and whack the ball.'

Negative thinking is enough to ruin even a great golfer. I had one 15-year-old student who absolutely bombed it, hitting the ball like a pro. He won several junior tournaments in California, shooting in the low 70s from the championship tees on challenging courses. Despite his success, though, the boy was obsessed with his bad shots. Even after good rounds, he only talked about the bad holes. 'I shot 73,' he would say, 'but I completely blew it when I tripled 17 and three-putted 18.'

Obviously, the young man had an attitude problem. His parents accentuated the situation by putting intense pressure on him to excel. It was heartbreaking to watch the boy's frustration build until he finally quit tournament golf. I'm glad that he quit, though, because he definitely wasn't having fun.

About a year after he quit, the boy returned to me for a lesson. His attitude had improved 100 per cent, and he was focusing almost exclusively on good shots and ignoring the bad ones. His parents' attitudes had dramatically changed, too, mellowing to the point where they didn't seem to care whether he shot 65 or 105. The boy returned to competition and became one of the top players on his high school team.

I OWNED HIM, FOR A WHILE

Tiger's famous punch, in which he jabs his right arm into the air several times in succession after hitting a great shot, isn't new. He's been doing it at least since he was six years old. I, too, used to punch the air after great shots, and I did a lot of punching when I played with Tiger because I got so excited whenever I had a chance to beat him.

Tiger and I had a heated rivalry, even when he was six. If I beat him in a putting contest or a nine-hole match, I didn't walk away and say, 'Nice playing.' I made sure to tell Tiger that I 'owned' him. And when he beat me, he said the same thing. Of course, I always tried to beat Tiger, because I knew that one day he would beat me on a regular basis.

We had a close match in Tennessee in August 1991. Tiger, then 15, had failed to qualify for match play in the US Amateur at the Honors Course, outside Chattanooga. Because he'd missed match play, we had a few extra days until our flights home, so Tiger, Earl, Kevin Woods (one of Tiger's older half brothers), Scott (one of the club's assistant pros) and I played two rounds together.

In one round, Tiger was two strokes ahead of me with one hole to play. Earl talked Tiger into hitting a driver on the tight 18th hole, a par 4. Tiger blocked the shot way right and the ball flew out of bounds. Tiger made a double-bogey, and after I drained a 15-footer for birdie I once again had come from behind to beat Tiger.

But my triumph was short-lived. The next day, Tiger dusted me by six shots, 72 to 78. While we were changing shoes in the parking lot after the round, Tiger smiled at me and said, 'I own you now, Rudy.'

'Yes, that's correct,' I said, deflated, knowing that my reign was over.

2. MY SIX KEY PRINCIPLES

There are six key principles I refer to in almost every lesson, whether the setting is a junior clinic or a one-on-one session. They are the principles you need to know to hit golf shots far and straight. Five of the ideas are swing-related concepts, and one idea covers equipment. Each concept is discussed in my five-step programme, but nowhere else in the book are these ideas presented as a single unit.

These six points are especially helpful for troubleshooting problems with your game. In most cases, the problem will be an incorrect execution of one of these points. Perhaps your clubs are improperly fitted, or you're out of balance while swinging, or you take too big a swing on a shot that requires a small swing.

When you do have a problem, the first place to look should be this list. Which of the six points is the problem related to? Approaching situations like this will help you root out the cause and find a reliable cure, rather than just putting on a plaster with a swing tip.

1. *Club fitting*: You need properly fitted equipment to hit a golf ball correctly. You can play decently without properly fitted gear, but you will definitely play better if you use properly fitted clubs. If you have limited resources and cannot afford a full set of well-fitted clubs, it is better to play with a less than full set of clubs and have every club fit, rather than use a complete set of clubs that do not fit correctly.

The most important aspect of club fitting is shaft length. The shaft's length needs to be appropriate for your height. The clubs' lie, shaft flex, swing weight and grip size are also important club-fitting factors. Chapter 10 provides a complete club-fitting discussion.

2. *Setup*: Also called the address position, the setup refers to your body's alignment to the target while you stand over the ball. The setup includes body posture, how you hold the club and the ball's position relative to your body. The setup should not be taken lightly because it's the foundation for your swing.

FOCUS ON CAUSE, NOT EFFECT

I don't dwell on negatives. If after hitting a poor shot a student asks, 'What did I do wrong?' I'll tell him, 'It doesn't matter what you did wrong. You should just focus on what you need to do correctly to hit a good shot.' Whatever mistake the student might have made is not relevant because it's the effect of a bad swing. The golfer must focus on what causes good shots.

3. *Motion equals power:* Not a lesson goes by that I don't tell the student, 'Motion equals power.' That's my favourite and most helpful mantra. The size of your motion, or swing, determines the amount of power a particular shot will have. A small motion – one in which the club doesn't go very far back or very far through after impact – is used for smaller shots. A big motion, in which you make a large body turn back and then through, is used for long shots, such as drives, bunker explosions, playing out of high grass or hitting the ball exceptionally high around the green.

Picture yourself standing in front of a big clock, with the clock at your back. At address, your club is at six o'clock, and your head is at twelve o'clock. You measure how far the club travels back and through by matching the position of your hands to the hours on the clock. A swing in which your hands travel back to seven o'clock and through to five o'clock will have less power than a backswing in which your hands go back to ten o'clock and through to two o'clock.

START BY SWINGING BIG

Beginners need to develop a full range of motion and have a large power base. These two things are closely related, and my advice about them applies to all golfers, regardless of age and body size. Range of motion is the size of a golfer's torso turn; in other words, the turning of the shoulders back away from the target and then back through towards the target. A golfer's power base is a measure of his range of motion. A small range of motion generates a small power base, and a big range of motion makes a big power base. To play good golf, and hit the ball far, you need a big power base.

Developing a big power base early in your golf career is a must, because it's very difficult to expand your power base after you've played the game for a few years. That's why I cringe whenever I hear, 'Swing nice and easy.'

Hitting far is good, and farther is better. Golf has become a power game, and short hitters are being left in the dust. Indeed, there's no substitute in golf for power, and the best way to make the ball go far is to develop a big power base. You can learn to control your power later, but you will have a very difficult time learning to add power.

Jack Nicklaus thinks first-time golfers need to swing with as much power as they can. He describes his ideas relating to power in his book My 55 Ways to Lower Your Score: *'The first thing I learned was to swing hard, and never mind where the ball went. That is the way Arnold Palmer was taught, too, and I think it is the right way.'*

Trying to maximise your power isn't just helpful. It's fun, because everybody loves to hit the ball far. But you need to learn that power isn't used exclusively with the driver from the tee. Power is essential on almost every shot.

4. *Balance equals control:* Staying in perfect balance throughout the swing gives you control. You control your golf ball with balance, not by keeping your head still or down, or by swinging easy. This concept applies to all shots, from putts

to drives. Few swings look alike on the professional tours, but all of the best players are in perfect balance during and after their swings. John Daly and Lee Trevino have very different swings. Daly has a very long motion in which the club travels well past parallel on the backswing and the follow-through, whereas Trevino has a very short backswing and follow-through. Despite the differences in their swings, both players are perfectly balanced in the finish position.

How can you tell if your balance is good? Hold your finish position after a swing. If you're balanced, somebody could give you a solid nudge with his or her hand and you would barely sway. However, if your balance isn't good, a solid nudge will make you sway or even fall down.

5. *Upper body turn:* Proper use of the upper body prevents the ball from going to the right. The upper body is the area that extends from the knees to the top of the head. Your upper body must continuously turn throughout every shot, excluding putts. At the start of the swing, your entire torso turns away from the target, and it continues rotating until the end of the backswing. After having turned back as far as necessary, you begin turning your torso in the opposite direction, back towards the target, and you continue turning until your belly button faces the target.

Think of the upper body turn as horizontally rotating your torso on top of your feet. That rotation provides power and moves the club. A common error in golf is to think that the arms swing the club. Incorrect. The upper body turn causes your torso, including the arms, to rotate, and that rotation swings the club, and that motion keeps the ball from going to the right.

6. *Lower body and the proper release:* Proper use of the lower body and a good release prevents the ball from hooking. The lower body is the area that extends from the knees to the

ground, and it supports the swing motion. The release is the slapping sensation of the club through the impact zone. You simply let your wrists and elbows bend as the club whips through the impact zone, slapping the ball from the side, similar to throwing a side-armed pitch in baseball or skimming a stone across a lake. This hitting from the side motion keeps the toe of the clubface from closing at impact and thus causing a hook. Your feet should remain flat, or grounded, which supports the swing motion. Never make any swing motion that compromises balance.

In the backswing, your weight should remain over, or barely inside, your right foot. Your weight gradually shifts from being over the right foot to over the left foot during the downswing. In the finish position, almost all of your weight should be centred over your left foot.

In the backswing and in the follow-through, don't let your weight sway outside where your feet are planted. It's helpful to imagine that during the swing you are standing inside a barrel. The barrel provides boundaries inside which you have to turn, and the boundaries help you to stay on top of your feet during the swing motion and not sway outside of your feet, which would cause you to be off balance. You should feel centred over your feet. Remember, staying on top of your feet and slapping the ball from the side keeps the ball from hooking.

3. THE PARENT'S PLACE

Today it's common to hear about overzealous parents throwing tantrums at their children's sporting events. Parents yell at their kids, the referees, the coaches and even other parents. One Florida athletic association now requires parents who want their children to play on one of the association's teams to go through a training programme aimed at preventing parental hysteria and violence. Parents have to watch a sportsmanship video, sign a code of ethics and vow not to cause disruptions at games.

Out-of-control parental behaviour at young people's sporting events has become so prevalent that the issue has been the subject of many cover stories like the one in *The New York Times* in May 2001. The article describes several communities that require parents to undergo training if they want to attend the youth league games in which their children participate. Describing the alarming frequency of 'sideline rage,' reporter Edward Wong writes, 'From hockey arenas in Maine to soccer fields in New Mexico, parents and amateur coaches are yelling and jeering – even spitting and brawling – as never before.'

Golf is not immune to overzealous behaviour. Sean O'Hair was one of the top juniors in the country in the late 1990s. His father, Mark, was always by his side, caddying, coaching and pushing his son to the limit. Mark would rouse his son for 5:30 a.m. workouts, and he made him run one mile for every stroke he shot above par in tournaments. Sean got $20 for every stroke he shot under par. It was Mark who convinced his son to turn pro after high school, and Sean, who probably could have earned a scholarship to play golf in college, was still toiling on the mini-tours at the end of 2001.

Sean's case is extreme, but it begs the question: where do parents fit into the golf learning equation? If it's possible, I think parents should be involved with their children's golf development. How involved they should be, though, depends on the individual family. Parents don't need to be golfers to provide positive support to their golf-playing kids, but I've seen strong parent-child relationships in which both the parents and the child play golf.

As for lessons, parents and their children both benefit by having one parent present during at least some of their son or daughter's instructional periods, whether those are group or private lessons. Parents who attend their children's lessons provide a comfort zone, making their kids more at ease and apt to perform well. This is especially true with student golfers who are ten years old and younger.

Another reason for parents to attend lessons, if they are familiar with the game, is so they can learn what the child is learning, and this helps the parents assist as 'coaches.' The parents don't have to give lessons; but by learning the same information their children are learning, parents can discuss the techniques and concepts with their youngsters when the pro is not available.

Parental involvement was at the core of the success I had with Tiger. Each of his parents provided support in different yet effective ways. Tiger's mother, Tida, was not involved in the day-to-day instruction because she didn't seriously play golf. Tida taught herself to play a passing level of golf because Tiger needed somebody to accompany him on the course during his elementary school days. Remember, Tiger was only four when he became serious about the game, and he wasn't allowed to play alone after school. His father, Earl, worked as a contract administrator at Boeing, and I couldn't always play with Tiger, so Tida filled that void.

Earl was an avid student of the game and enjoyed learning information about the game and swing technique. He usually accompanied Tiger to his weekend lessons with me. In doing so, Earl learned to be a better player himself. It's easy to see how, in this environment, Earl's understanding of the swing enabled him to give Tiger helpful advice when he needed it.

PENALTY STROKES = GOOD BEHAVIOUR

Giving penalty shots for doing things other than breaking the Rules of Golf is a great way to make kids behave when you're playing or practising with them. I set ground rules when I'm on the course with kids, doling out penalties for breaking rules of etiquette. It's funny how children will do almost anything to avoid penalty strokes, even in casual rounds. I also give out penalties, to be added to a child's score during a round, for bad behaviour while I'm transporting kids to the golf course.

Tiger was so good that he rarely needed the full hour I usually set aside for his lessons. Tiger and I would work together for about a half hour, and then I'd stop working with Tiger and move to where Earl was hitting and begin focusing my attention on his swing. Earl usually needed more swing help than Tiger.

That turned out to be a blessing, and I wish I could work with every parent as closely as I did with Earl. Not only did Earl's game improve, but Tiger's did, too, in large part because Earl was able to discuss many of the same concepts with Tiger that Tiger and I had worked on. In golf, parents are often the real full-time teachers of their children because they spend more time with their kids than the teacher does. The teacher might be with the child for an hour or two a week, but the parent lives with the child and has more time to share instructional concepts. That's why I like to have both the parent and the child as students.

Earl and Tida had another motive for being involved with Tiger's golf, and that was to provide solid support for their son. They were never concerned about Tiger's score. They didn't care what he shot or how he finished in competitions. They only wanted to know if he was having fun and learning.

KEEPING IT ALL IN PERSPECTIVE

Earl and Tida Woods were supportive of their son, but they never pushed him to play golf. They always kept golf in perspective. Tida was available to take Tiger to practice and tournaments, but school always came first. Tiger was permitted to play whenever he wanted, but only after he'd finished his homework.

It's fine to drop off your child at the golf course if he or she is working with a teacher or participating in a junior clinic. Some eight- and nine-year-olds are mature enough so their parents can leave them at the course and they will practise on their own and stay out of trouble. But I discourage parents from simply dumping their kids at the course without any supervision or pre-planned activity for them to participate in. Tiger enjoyed playing and practising alone, even when he was as young as six, but he still needed adult supervision at that young age.

MUM AND DAD, LEAVE THE BAGGAGE AT HOME

Very often adults try to encourage young people, but they often end up limiting the kids' performances by imposing their own values and experiences. Just because something is difficult for an adult to learn doesn't mean it has to be difficult for a younger person. That's why you should never say, 'Don't hit a driver to a narrow fairway.' Why not? To some golfers, the fairway won't look skinny. Canadian tour pro Moe Norman used to say, 'If the ball fits, why not hit a driver?'

If I had told Tiger how difficult it was for me to master some parts of golf, he could have become so discouraged that he might have quit the game. I tried very hard never to impose my views on him or any of my other students, and my positive attitude rubbed off. What I find most amazing about Tiger is that even at a very young age, he didn't care about how other people played golf. The only thing on his mind was his ball, his clubs and the swing he needed to put his ball into the hole.

Tiger's not interested in following in somebody else's foot-steps. He's one of the most intense athletes in the world, but he doesn't much care what his competition does. He thinks about his own game, because he knows that if he performs as well as he can, he has a good chance to win.

LET KIDS DO IT THEIR WAY

Kids will work hard if they are having fun. Golf is unlike most other sports, because everybody can play like a pro. Well, maybe not everybody can hit it as long as a pro, but most people can make the same score on a given hole. That's what makes golf unique. If you are ten years old, you are going to have a hard time hitting a baseball 385 feet for a home run, but it's well within your ability to hit a 125-yard shot to a par 3 green and hole a putt for a birdie. Golf is perhaps the only sport in which pulling off the seemingly impossible is possible for everybody. It's one of the only games in which a child can, on occasion, hit the ball as well as a tour professional.

Youthful students may not, however, work hard at what they are 'supposed' to work on. I have a very talented 12-year-old student, and his father recognises his son's talent and encourages him to work hard on his swing technique. But his son doesn't care about technique. He just wants to play golf. And when his dad insists that he hit balls to work on his swing, he just goes through the motions, which is no fun for him, his instructor or his father.

GOLF OVER SOCCER? NO CONTEST

A father recently asked if I would give private lessons to his six-year-old daughter. The girl had started playing golf when she was four, and she had had some lessons from other teachers before coming to me. She had a nice swing, she made solid contact on almost every shot, and I saw lots of potential. However, her dad told me that his daughter wasn't progressing as quickly as he felt she should be.

I'm always wary of parents who are so result-oriented, especially when I'm dealing with a very young student. But I kept my mouth shut in this instance, and I agreed to schedule the first lesson. While her father sat in the background, the girl and I had one of the most positive sessions I've ever experienced. She fell into a groove, and with only a few pointers – 'Balance equals control' and 'Whack the ball' – she was hitting the ball great.

OK, she topped a few balls and five-putted a few times on the practice green, but she also hit a lot of terrific shots. More important, she smiled throughout the lesson.

A few days after the lesson, the girl's father called to schedule another lesson. He was ecstatic, and said, 'My daughter had so much fun that she wants to give up soccer so she can practise golf and do better the next time she sees you.'

IN EVERY KID THERE LURKS A TIGER

At four, Tiger had as good a swing as I had ever seen, and I'm not just talking about kids. Tiger was a miniature tour pro. As awesome as his swing was, Tida's little boy had an attitude that was equally, if not more, impressive. He addressed a golf ball with supreme confidence and poise. He also had an uncanny ability to forget bad shots.

Most children refuse to limit themselves or get depressed over one bad swing. Adults, however, do limit themselves, and they often try to limit youngsters, even if they do so inadvertently. When I ask young students if they think that they're making progress, even if it's their first or second lesson, they almost always answer, 'Yes!' Kids tend to think they're good at golf, until adults convince them that they're not good. Golfers shouldn't be told, 'That's good, but you can do better.' They should simply be told 'Good shot' or nothing at all. Telling a student that he or she can 'do better' is another way of telling him that he's no good.

I never dwell on bad shots when I'm working with a pupil, young or old. 'That's OK,' I'll say after a student tops or misses a shot. Then I might add, 'What do you need to feel to hit your good shot?' I like to dwell on what a person needs to do to be successful.

4. HOW TO USE MY FIVE-STEP PROGRAMME

My five-step programme has evolved significantly since I started teaching it about 25 years ago. The programme Tiger participated in during the early 1980s contained the same basic information as my programme contains today, but the concepts have been significantly refined and better organised.

My programme, which never strays from the basics, is purposely uncomplicated, and it's designed to provide a learning environment in which students can develop their abilities to the fullest and have fun in the process. Early on, the programme consisted primarily of weekly hour-long group lessons that were followed by stroke-play tournaments. For Tiger and other kids, the combination of the lessons and the weekly tournaments was the foundation for developing the programme I have today.

The present programme is organised around four separate disciplines. They are (1) Putting, (2) Less-than-Full Swing, (3) Full Swing and (4) General Knowledge. Each of the disciplines has five steps, or levels. By progressing at a comfortable pace through each of the four disciplines, you'll learn the fundamentals of hitting the ball, how to maximise your enjoyment of the game, and the game's jargon and rules.

READ THE ENTIRE BOOK FIRST

I suggest you read this entire book before starting any of the work in the disciplines. I call this learning process 'The whole picture – the partial picture – the whole picture.' That means you first gain a feel for my entire teaching philosophy, so when you go back and work on the specifics you'll know how they fit into the big picture. Another reason to read the whole book first is because the quizzes in Chapter 8 (General Knowledge) include information from the entire book.

Each step has an objective, a lesson and a skill requirement that you should achieve before beginning the next step. There are also drills sprinkled throughout the disciplines. You should study the lessons and practise, and when you feel that you've mastered the technique, you're ready to attempt the skill requirement. Even if you learn the lesson in a given step quickly, I recommend that you practise it for a couple of weeks before trying the skill requirement and, if you succeed, then move to the next step. Take your time and have fun.

My programme provides enough information so that if you know absolutely nothing about golf, and if you just happened to be shipwrecked on a desert island with a golf course and had some golf equipment, you could learn to play excellent golf using this book. The amount of time you take to complete the programme is irrelevant. More important, you should give yourself enough time to absorb the concepts and develop a feel for the swing.

I suggest you take the 'desert island' approach to learning golf with my programme. By that I mean avoid listening to tips and techniques from other sources. I'm definitely not the only good golf instructor, but you'll be confused if you mix my ideas with the concepts of other teachers. The only thing I can't provide is desire. As I've said, golf is easy, but it takes work to become a good golfer. The work, though, can be fun.

If you're a parent, please understand that you don't have to be an expert to use this programme to teach golf to your children (or to yourself). Kids have a knack for absorbing information. They don't need encyclopaedias of factoids explained by a master guru – nor do most kids want that. Kids need the basics presented in a positive and happy atmosphere. As parents, there's a lot you can do to foster this atmosphere.

NO KNOWLEDGE, GREAT SWING

Tiger was an awesome golfer at age five, but he didn't know anything specific about the swing. He already had been playing golf for a couple of years, but he had had very little technical

training. He had learned to swing by copying his father, Earl;
by mimicking good players he saw either in person or on
television; and by experimenting on his own.

Tiger learned to play golf the way most children learn to play
baseball – by copying others, not through tedious training under
the close eye of a coach. Of course, Earl helped Tiger in golf
along the way, but Earl did not have a sophisticated
understanding of swing mechanics. Nevertheless, the concepts
he shared with his little boy were wonderfully simple. That's the
way every beginner – regardless of age – should learn to play
golf, and I hope you'll pattern your family's golf experience on
that of the Woodses.

The importance of relying on the 'less is more' concept to
teach golf to young people and beginners is one of the most
valuable lessons I've learned during my career as an instructor.
Before I met Tiger, I thought that you needed lots of knowledge
to be a good golfer. But Tiger, at age five, had almost no golf
knowledge, and yet he was a tiny Mozart in spikes. Parents
should do their best to assure that their children start learning
the game in a pure and uncluttered mental environment. As one
grows in the game, understanding and knowledge will grow, too.
Just be patient. Don't push information on anybody, or be
rushed to learn the nuances of the swing. Learn at a natural pace.

I can't stress enough how important it is to avoid information
overload. Adults often want to fix a problem or improve a skill
by throwing more knowledge at it. But doing that never solves
the problem. If you don't believe me, listen to this story about
the late golf instructor Harvey Penick.

A top PGA Tour player went back to his long-time coach, Mr
Penick, for a lesson. This man had been playing terribly. He felt
like he couldn't hit a fairway or make a putt. Before the slump,
though, he'd been a star on the Tour. 'Mr Penick, I'm lost,' he
said on the practice tee.

Mr Penick suggested that the golfer start the lesson by hitting
some shots. Nothing more. Club selection didn't matter. The
golfer obliged, and began by swinging an iron. Mr Penick sat in

a chair behind the student, observing closely but saying nothing. The golfer hit some decent shots and some not-so-decent shots, then turned around.

'Any suggestions, Mr Penick?' he said.

Dead silence. Mr Penick just sat there. The golfer knew what that meant. Mr Penick had nothing to say just yet, so the golfer again started hitting. To his surprise, his shots were getting progressively better. He started feeling good about his swing. After 30 minutes, with still not a peep from the guru, the golfer was hitting the ball great, but he was also frustrated. He wanted to hear something, anything, from Mr Penick. After all, he'd made a long trip to see him because his game was a wreck. Nevertheless, the golfer respected Mr Penick too much to say what he was thinking: 'I'm in the worst slump of my life, and you're not giving me an ounce of help!'

By the time the golfer had finished the session, dripping with sweat, Mr Penick hadn't said a word. But the golfer's frustration had vanished; he felt like a new man. His swing was grooved, and he was striping the ball as well as ever. The golfer had found his groove without any new information. Soon after the lesson, the golfer returned to the PGA Tour and won a tournament.

I love that story because it underscores my most important beliefs about learning golf. The PGA Tour player had come to Mr Penick in dire straits, hoping for some knowledge to fix his swing; but that's not what he needed, and Mr Penick was smart enough to know that. All the player needed was to get back into his comfort zone, to become reacquainted with his swing and his feel. Hitting shots on the practice tee in front of his old coach did the trick. He didn't need the major repairs he had thought would be necessary. That is often the case, although students have a hard time believing it.

Generally, a little extra practice with the basics will be enough to get you back on track. Of course, that's not always true, but it is true more often than not. If a bird flaps its wings but doesn't immediately take off, the bird doesn't get new wings. It keeps flapping, and eventually it flies away.

IF AT FIRST YOU DON'T SUCCEED, TRY AGAIN

The primary reason I developed my junior programme was to provide something for kids that I never had: golf instruction designed primarily for kids in an organised programme. My first foray into junior golf was at Hasley Canyon Golf Course in Saugus, California, in 1971, a few years before I tried to succeed as a tour player. Back then I ran a six-week programme in which each session focused on a different element of the swing. At the time, I didn't understand that I should have been teaching kids how to play the game, not just how to swing a club.

My programme seemed like a logical way to teach golf, but it wasn't successful. I didn't work out the reason for a few years, but it finally hit me like a brick falling out of the sky. Children have too many activities to commit to six consecutive sessions. If a student missed one of my group sessions, he or she had no chance to learn the subject we had discussed, and was often unprepared for the next lesson. As a result, I was doing too many make-up lessons, and lots of kids were still lost because they'd missed the previous week's session and didn't know what I was talking about. It was confusing for the other instructors as well, and it was a scheduling nightmare for the parents.

I knew I had to modify the programme because it wasn't working – except for the few kids who had perfect attendance. The solution seems simple today, but it took a lot of thinking to discover. I don't recall precisely why, but I decided to copy the scheduling format used in schools, in which students are typically divided into grades, and each day students get small doses of a variety of subjects. Trying to absorb all the knowledge on a given topic in one day would be overwhelming, to say the least. But if you learn a little each day from each discipline, the schooling is manageable and fun.

By applying this building-block approach to teaching golf, I created a five-step programme that covers the fundamental disciplines of golf and provides the skills necessary to hit every possible shot. The steps are based on skill level, from Step 1 (beginner) to Step 5 (a bona fide golfer).

Along with each step, there is a test which the student should be able to pass before advancing to the next step. For the Less-than-Full Swing, Full Swing and Putting topics, the tests are skills-oriented exams that should be done in a practice area and on the course. The General Knowledge tests are written ones. All of the tests identify a basic level of competency or knowledge a pupil should have before progressing to the next step.

I hope you have fun with the tests. Don't worry if you don't pass one. That's fine. It happens to many of my students. Study the ideas for the topic some more, practise, and take the test again. You will succeed.

When my instructors and I teach the programme, we give students a little bit of each discipline at every session, including elements of Putting, Less-than-Full Swing, Full Swing and General Knowledge. That provides balanced exposure to all facets of the game, and it also creates a natural outline for the sessions. Some students have relatively short attention spans, so breaking up each lesson into four parts maintains enough interest for children not to get tired or bored.

I suggest scheduling at least one practice session a week. Two sessions a week are better, but that's not always possible. Each practice session should last between 60 and 90 minutes, allowing for short breaks between each discipline. The suggested times are suitable for students of all ages. I have several eight- and nine-year-old students who never lose interest during a 90-minute session. They rarely get bored because they shift between disciplines every 20 minutes, and doing that provides enough variety to hold anyone's attention.

Before starting a session, it's a good idea to plan your time. Divide the session into four equal parts, allowing for short breaks between each discipline. As mentioned above, if you have 90 minutes, you might want to devote 20 minutes to each discipline. Working a little on each discipline in every session is best, because you do all the things you'd normally do in a complete round of golf.

If things don't go well with one of the disciplines, don't be concerned. You're not supposed to hit a hundred perfect shots in a row. Move on to the next discipline and forget about the past. The goal is not to perfect a discipline in one session. It's to work on the different disciplines consistently, maintaining a positive attitude. Over time you'll notice improvement. At school, you don't remain in your maths class until you're an algebra expert. Rather, you regularly go to class, and each day you make small steps forward. Hopefully, by the end of the term, you've mastered the subject. The same principle applies to learning golf.

TAKE IT ONE LEVEL AT A TIME

Talking about golf is an essential part of learning how to enjoy and play the game. That's why I suggest that learning golfers get together on a regular basis and talk about golf. Talk about anything – your favourite players; shots you love to hit or shots you want to learn to hit; stories about great matches you've been involved in or watched on TV. The subject doesn't matter, as long as it's about golf.

Perhaps you will excel at three disciplines within a given step and be weak in the fourth discipline. You may be tempted to skip that discipline and return to it later. Don't do it. You'll probably forget that you skipped the discipline, so returning to it is unlikely. What's more, while the four disciplines are different, the five different steps within each discipline are designed to work together and complement each other.

Don't forget: the premise of my programme is to teach students how to play golf by the rules and on their own. That's why you need to master each step in each of all four disciplines.

WHAT YOU NEED TO BEGIN MY PROGRAMME

You need an honest desire and a willingness to learn the game of golf. You also need equipment, but it doesn't have to be expensive. There's nothing wrong with having brand-name gear – irons, shoes, balls and other gizmos. But remember: it's the archer, not the arrow, that hits the golf ball. Any tour professional could whip you – and me – with just about any equipment, no matter how old it is. Don't get mesmerised by seductive advertising slogans – or zealous friends – that passionately claim that clubs, balls and other gear can make you play better.

To go through my programme, and to play golf, you need just a few clubs. It's fine if your set includes only a putter, a short iron, a mid-iron and a fairway wood. You can learn golf and play it very well with only those four clubs, as long as they fit you properly. Having more clubs is helpful, but by no means mandatory. You'll also need balls. You can buy new balls, but used models will perform just as well, and they're less expensive. Some golfers prefer playing with a glove, but you don't need one. Many professionals, including Fred Couples and Bob Estes, don't wear a glove when they play golf. Another requirement is a copy of the *Rules of Golf*, the game's official rulebook.

In a nutshell, here's what you need to begin my five-step programme.

1. Clubs: a minimum of four (putter, 9-iron, 5-iron, fairway wood)
2. Balls
3. Golf glove (optional)
4. Golf shoes (optional)
5. A copy of the *Rules of Golf*
6. Desire and a willingness to learn
7. Imagination
8. A smile

HOW GOOD CAN YOU BECOME?

There's more than enough information in my programme for you to become a great golfer. It's happened before, with Tiger, LPGA player Amy Fruhwirth, touring professional Roger Tambellini and the past few Atascadero High School boys' golf teams. Those are just a few of the star golfers who've grown up on my programme. Working with the programme provides an environment rich with possibility. The only question is how hard you want to work and what you want to achieve.

But no matter how hard you work and what your goals are, there is no guarantee that you or your child will become a tour player. My motive has never been to create a flock of superstars. I strive to provide a fun learning environment in which golfers can learn to enjoy the game and play it competently, by the rules and at a good pace. Anything else is icing on the cake.

HOW LONG WILL IT TAKE TO GO THROUGH THE PROGRAMME?

A six-year-old could master the five steps within a year, or she could take three years. With weekly one-hour sessions, an 11-year-old starting from scratch would probably complete the programme within a year. No matter how long it takes, though, stick with the programme until you can play golf by the rules and at the proper pace.

After finishing my programme, it will be time to assess your ambitions. Do you want to continue studying the game? Or continue to play the game with the skills you've developed to this point? Both options are great. If you want to continue studying, I recommend finding an LPGA or PGA teaching pro in your home town.

Regardless of your goal, I suggest that after completing the final part of each step in my programme, you focus your free time at the course on utilising the exercises in Chapter 12 (Imagination and creativity) and on playing the games in Chapter 9.

HOW DID I NAME THIS BOOK?

The title, *In Every Kid There Lurks a Tiger*, echoes the essence of my programme. I've never had a student who wasn't a fierce competitor or who didn't enjoy success on the golf course. It doesn't matter whether you're a 32 handicapper or a scratch player. Everybody wants to play well, improve and have fun, and those motives drive people to practise.

That doesn't mean every child wants to be a professional and win ten major championships. But all students want to hit the ball correctly, and they're eager to learn how to do it. What I like most about teaching is seeing that faint but sure smile on a student's face after he or she's made solid contact for the first time. It makes me come back day after day, lesson after lesson. In every child, and adult, there is a competitor who wants to enjoy golf and fulfil her or his potential.

PROGRAMME CHECKLIST

Use this checklist to track your progress as you advance through the programme. And once again, please don't rush. The goal is to learn to play golf. It's not to finish the programme as soon as possible.

Every time you finish a step within one of the four disciplines, place a check mark (or an *X*) in the box for that step. When you have checks in a level of steps for each discipline, you should move on to the next step.

Good luck, and have some serious fun!

RUDY DURAN'S 5-STEP PROGRAMME

	STEP 1	STEP 2	STEP 3	STEP 4	STEP 5
Putting					
Less-than-Full Swing					
Full Swing					
General Knowledge					

5. PUTTING
THE MORE YOU PUTT, THE BETTER YOU'LL PUTT

A SIMPLE ACT MADE COMPLICATED

Putting is one of the simplest acts in golf. Yet for many people putting can be the most vexing and complicated part of the game. Putting has confounded some of golf's all-time greats, including Ben Hogan and Johnny Miller. Hogan eventually became so distraught over putting that he said it should be abolished. He suggested that greens should be replaced by huge funnels that would stretch to the following tees. Approach shots would land in the funnel and roll to the next tee so you'd be ready to play the next hole without ever having struck a putt.

Putting has been analysed by players and teachers to the nth degree. There are also some very hefty books devoted solely to putting. But putting is not that complicated. A seven-year-old novice can, on any given hole, putt as well as a 35-five-year-old tour professional. Putting is about feel and touch, and it doesn't require much power. It requires you to survey the green to determine how the ball will curve; select a target; and then hit the ball with the proper amount of power. You don't have to worry about wind or club choice or even about your stroke. There's no perfect putting style; just be sure, no matter how you stand, that you're in perfect balance. In putting, as in other parts of the game, 'Balance equals control.'

Here's how to putt, in a nutshell. Get comfortable over the ball, select a target, hit the ball squarely towards the target and keep on hitting the ball until it falls into the cup. Think about putting in those simple terms, and I guarantee that you'll be a decent putter, maybe even an excellent putter. How good will you be? The more you putt, the better you'll get.

Lost in a sea of mental confusion on the greens, golfers often forget to hone in on the basics: the line you want the ball to start on and the power it needs to have it end up in the hole.

Confusion about putting stems from a major misunderstanding. Putting is not hitting the ball into the hole. Putting is what you do up to and during the act of hitting the ball. Everything that happens after you hit the ball is out of your control.

My contention – that the act of putting actually ends after you hit the ball – is radical. It's difficult, I realise, to block out what happens *after* you hit the ball. But you've got to understand this concept or you'll never be a good putter. In golf, you can only control what happens up to the point of impact.

FIRST-TIME PUTTERS

I love teaching young children to putt because their minds are uncluttered, devoid of the false beliefs with which adults often get overwhelmed. Kids don't bring unnecessary baggage to the course, and for them, putting is the easiest way to play like a pro.

Should you offer a beginner technical advice when he or she is putting for the first time? No! Simply place a few balls on the green, give the novice a putter and ask him or her to hit some putts to a hole. Don't provide any extra information, like how to stand, how to grip the putter or how to swing. Let the new student do what comes naturally. If he or she hits the ball 20 feet past the hole, it's OK. Say something positive, like, 'Just keep hitting the ball until it goes in the hole.' The only advice I recommend sharing with a novice is this: 'Fewer strokes is better than more strokes.'

Indeed, my approach has helped produce many good putters over the last thirty years. As people continue to develop their game, adjustments may be necessary, such as altering the length of the backswing and follow-through, moving the ball position at address and changing the style of putter. But do yourself a favour: don't get bogged down in details. I've seen many people turn putting into a lifelong science project, and consequently lose all ability to get the ball into the hole.

WHICH PUTTER IS BEST FOR YOU?

There are hundreds of putter styles. There are long putters, pit putters, belly-button putters, two-way putters, offset putters, heel-toe balanced putters, centre- and heel-shafted putters, mallet putters and blade putters, to name just a few. Arnold Palmer once owned over 3,000 putters. In fact, you don't even have to putt with a putter. I've seen people putt – and putt well – with sand wedges and 3-woods.

Why do so many putters exist? Not for the good of the game, but for the good of the club manufacturers, who sell millions of dollars worth of putters annually in the United States alone. Golfers always have, and always will, believe that a slight modification in putting technique or equipment will make a huge difference in the results. Sadly, this is not true. Perhaps you'll see a short-term improvement when you pick up a new putter, but the only way to putt better is to practise. No club can make you a better putter.

That said, I'm the first one to admit that I am not immune to the search for the perfect putter, because I, too, frequently change putters. I know my quest won't make me a better putter. I've owned dozens of putters, and I've putted well with all of them and badly with all of them.

My advice is to change putters for fun, and if you can afford to change. Otherwise, get the least expensive putter you can find that feels and looks good, practise all day and all night, and you'll be an awesome putter.

Lee Trevino proved beyond reasonable doubt that you can putt well with almost any putter. Years ago, at a tournament in Europe, he bought an inexpensive putter at the pro shop. He liked the putter, but he wasn't quite satisfied with the way it looked, so he banged it against the pavement to make it look exactly like he wanted. Trevino won that tournament.

IS THERE A PERFECT PUTTING TECHNIQUE?

The first time I saw Tiger putt, he already had good feel and an ability to propel the ball the proper distance and on his intended line. Was his technique perfect? That depends on how you define *perfect*. His stroke might not have been as aesthetically pleasing as the stroke belonging to Brad Faxon, who led the PGA Tour in putting three different years, from 1996 to

2000. But Tiger had nearly perfect technique in the ways that count most: his ball either went into the hole most of the time, or stopped close to it. Because Tiger was so effective on the greens, I simply let his stroke evolve throughout our years together, giving him little pointers along the way, like 'Hold your follow-through,' and 'Be sure to hit the ball solid.'

Jack Nicklaus stands hunched over the ball. Nancy Lopez stands very erect. Despite their different styles, both Lopez and Nicklaus are excellent putters. One of the most important things to keep in mind while putting is to maintain the same address position on all putts. Repetition is essential to good putting, and you can't develop a repetitive stroke if you're always changing your technique.

No two people stand exactly alike on the green. However, all great putters look natural when they're standing over a putt, and their strokes are usually smooth, pendulum-like and even in size, going back approximately the same distance that they go forward. The pendulum motion can be wristy, like Billy Casper, or non-wristy, like Loren Roberts. Another style is 'pop' putting. In that technique, the golfer draws the putter back a long way and then stops the putter almost immediately after making contact. Gary Player is a pop putter.

Imagine if Casper, Player and Roberts had been told to change their putting technique, forced to conform to what a teacher considered ideal. They might not have become great putters. Fortunately, though, they have stayed true to their individual styles. As long as the ball rolls straight off the putter face and has the proper speed, I would never change a golfer's technique.

I know lots of people who have good putting ability but are never satisfied with their putting. Instead, they're constantly looking for nirvana, a putting style that will make them drain every putt. They copy the style used by the latest PGA Tour winner, or that of a recent playing partner who putted well. The result is that they never putt as well as they could.

ALL PUTTS ARE STRAIGHT PUTTS
All putts are straight putts. Everywhere, all the time. Regardless of the length of the putt or how much the slope of the green

will curve the ball, the ball *always* leaves the clubface on a straight line. You can only control what happens at the beginning of a putt, and every putt rolls straight at the beginning. After that, the green takes control of the ball.

You only have control over hitting the ball straight off the clubface with a certain amount of power. Learning to launch the ball on a straight line off the clubface and hitting with the right amount of power are the only putting techniques you need to learn. If you can master these two skills, you'll be an awesome putter.

DRILL: THROUGH THE GATE

When I putt, my target is a spot about 3 inches ahead of the ball. I know I can hit it to that spot every time, and if I've correctly gauged the power, the ball will almost always go into the hole.

My favourite putting drill is to put two coins on the green a few inches ahead of my ball and on the line I want to hit the ball. The coins should be 2 inches apart, forming a little gate through which you want to hit the ball. Hit putts of varying lengths and curves, using the gate – not the hole – as your target.

Putting through the gate reduces putting to its basic elements, and it helps you to avoid worrying about all the open space between you and the hole. After lining up the putt, all you need to think about is the space between your ball and the gate.

DISTANCE, DISTANCE, DISTANCE

Great putters concentrate almost exclusively on hitting the ball the proper distance. If they start the ball on the correct line (hit it through the imaginary gate) and have correctly judged the power necessary to hit the ball to the hole, the ball will often go in.

One of the best putters in the world, Loren Roberts has been called the 'Boss of the Moss' by his peers. Loren grew up in my home town, San Luis Obispo, California, and we've played a few rounds together. Every single putt Loren hits looks like it is going in the hole, whether he is 2 feet or 50 feet away from the hole.

Loren has a tremendous sense of confidence and poise on the greens that he developed through an enormous amount of practice. He worked as an assistant professional at San Luis Obispo Country Club in the late 1970s. The club had patio lights that were so bright they illuminated the practice putting green, and after work Loren often practised putting late into the evening.

Loren concentrates almost totally on distance when practising his putting. He hits putts that are short (less than 6 feet) and long (over 20 feet) and almost nothing in between. The short putts help him develop confidence that he can launch his ball straight off the putter face every time, and the long putts develop distance control. If the world's best putter focuses on only two basic concepts, shouldn't you, too?

How do you adjust distance? Technically, by adjusting the speed of the club head. Realistically, though, you're not a machine, and nobody can precisely programme the speed at which they swing a golf club. So judging distance comes down to 'feel' and instincts, which you develop through practice.

READING GREENS

Were you born knowing how to read a book? No. You learned to read by practising, and it took a lot of practice to read as well as you do today. Reading golf greens is similar. Nobody just knows how to read a green. However, everybody can learn how to read one.

Reading greens involves determining how the slope of the ground will curve the ball. Remember, the ground – not your stroke – curves the ball. Some putts proceed along a straight line to the hole, meaning you aim directly at the hole, but most putts have at least a little curve, and it's your job to determine how much curve a putt will have.

If the ground is higher on the right side of the intended line as you face the hole than it is on the left side, the ball will curve down the hill, from right to left, as it rolls towards the hole. In order to get the ball into the hole, you'll have to aim to the right of the hole. How far to the right depends on how hard you hit the ball. If you hit the ball hard, it will curve less than if you hit it gently.

For the most part, you'll learn how to read greens through experience. As you progress through each step of my programme, your green-reading ability will improve. Don't expect to read greens perfectly at the beginning, but don't be surprised if you can.

Here are a few green-reading tips.

1. Look for the highest ground in the immediate area of the green. The ball curves away from the highest to the lowest point. As you face the hole, if Mt Everest is on your right and a valley is on your left, your ball will probably curve from right to left, away from Mt Everest and towards the valley.
2. Visualise which way water would flow if you dumped a bucket of water on the green between your ball and the hole. The direction in which the water would flow is the direction the ball will roll.
3. Watch other people's putts. This is the best way to read a green. People make mistakes. Balls don't. If your partner's ball rolls in a certain direction, the odds are 100 per cent that your ball will roll that way too, if you are on the same line. Golfers call this copycat technique 'Going to school' or 'Getting a teach'. It's legal according to the *Rules of Golf*.

Here are the five steps for putting.

STEP 1: Rolling the ball
STEP 2: Alignment
STEP 3: Pre-shot routine
STEP 4: Own your stroke
STEP 5: Practice, practice, practice

STEP 1: ROLLING THE BALL

Objective: To become proficient at hitting the ball so it stops in or near the hole.

Lesson: Take one ball and your putter to a practice putting green. First, we're going to discuss gripping the putter.

Pick up the putter and hold it with both hands on the grip so the clubhead is sitting lightly on the ground behind the ball. It doesn't matter where your hands are on the grip. Just be sure that they feel comfortable.

You have two basic options with the grip. Your left hand can be below the right hand, or your left hand can be above the right hand. Your hands can be close together or far apart, touching or not touching. The best way to find out which grip works best for you is to experiment and practise.

One of the country's best golf teachers, Jim McLean, suggests that students who have trouble on the greens should putt differently on every hole during a round. Some people who putt differently on every hole do as well, if not better, than putting with their regular style for 18 consecutive holes. This exercise shows that there are many ways to hold a putter and still hit good putts. You need to find which way works best for you and stick with it.

I suggest that students begin putting with a putter that has a standard-length shaft. I don't suggest students start by using an extra-long putter because I think you have better feel with a standard-length putter. Standard putters are closer in length to the rest of the clubs in your bag, and beginners are often more used to handling clubs of that size. Don't get me wrong; I'm not against long putters. In fact, I occasionally use one. But I suggest you learn to putt with a standard-length putter and switch later if you feel like experimenting.

EVEN GRIP PRESSURE

Grip pressure is how hard you hold the club. There's no formula for grip pressure because grip pressure can't easily be

*quantified. I give students two ways to understand proper grip
pressure. The first is that grip pressure should be even, from
finger to finger in the grip, and throughout the stroke. The
second is that you should hold the putter 'more light than tight'.
You should use the same pressure with a putter as you would
use to hold a child's hand while crossing the street. You don't
hold the child's hand so tight that he cries, but you don't hold it
so loose that he can run away.*

Your goal in Step 1 is to learn to get the ball rolling forwards
by hitting it squarely with the putter. To become proficient at
this, you need to hit hundreds of putts, of varying distances,
solely aiming to make solid contact. Solid contact occurs when
you hit the ball with the centre of the clubface, which is called
the sweet spot. Don't worry too much about line or distance
right now.

After establishing your ideal grip and stance, you're ready to
begin hitting putts. Stand 6 feet from a hole with flat ground
between you and the hole. Take your address position and grip
the putter. Don't worry about anything except making sure that
the putter feels comfortable in your hands and that you feel
comfortable standing over the ball. We'll deal with specifics later.

Look back and forth, from the hole to the ball, a couple of
times to see where you want to hit the ball, and then pick out
a spot a few inches ahead of the ball. That spot, not the hole,
is your target. If you roll the ball over the spot with the proper
power, the ball should go into the hole.

Now hit the ball off the putter so it rolls over the spot and,
hopefully, into the hole. If it doesn't go in, move to where the
ball is now and hit it again. Don't pick up your ball and start
over. After you've put the ball in the cup, remove it and select
another hole. The second hole should be 30 feet or more away
from you. Again, hit the ball until it goes in the hole. Don't start
over, but hit from where the ball stops rolling. You can't start
over in real golf, so get used to hitting the ball until you hole out.

I suggest hitting only one ball at a time until it goes into the
hole. Some players often hit lots of putts from the same spot, or

make a circle around the hole with lots of balls and try to knock each ball in. Don't try these drills yet.

DISTANCE CONTROL

When putting, the club's backswing and follow-through should be approximately the same size. If your backswing is 2 feet long, your follow-through should be 2 feet as well. Having a backswing and a follow-through of equal lengths helps to create a consistent rhythm throughout your stroke.

Here's a drill to practise if most of your putts are rolling too far or too short. Put a ball on the green 6 inches from the hole. Hit the ball into the cup. Retrieve the ball, and hit it in again from the same spot. After you've hit five putts in a row into the hole from 6 inches, put the ball 9 inches from the hole. Make five in a row. If you miss a putt, you have to start over. After 9 inches, move to 15 inches and make five in a row.

This drill forces you to hit a lot of shots in a short period of time, with your sole focus on making solid contact. Since the putts are short, this will help you adjust the speed of the club to the correct distance. Hitting with the proper amount of power will gradually become instinctive.

Be sure to use only one ball in this drill, and to treat each putt as if you had never seen it before. That means you should step away from the ball after every putt, and establish a new address position for each shot. This may seem redundant, but repetition is a great way to develop better distance control. Taking your address position and lining up for every putt in practice is the only way to prepare for playing real golf.

You're ready to go back to playing holes on the putting green after doing this drill three times in a row. That means you drain five consecutive 6-inch putts, five straight 9-inch putts and then five 15-inchers in a row.

Skill requirement: Your goal is to average five or fewer putts per hole for a nine-hole putting round on a practice green, incorporating a mix of short (6 feet or less) and long holes (20 feet or more). You've completed

Step 1 after having shot 45 or better per round for three nine-hole putting rounds.

STEP 2: ALIGNMENT

Objective: At address, to have your putter pointed in the direction you want the ball to start rolling.

Lesson: It doesn't matter where your body faces while you putt. It does matter, however, where your putter faces. It's impossible to putt well if the clubhead is pointed anywhere except where you want the ball to start rolling. The first step on the road to good putting is making sure the clubhead is aimed at the target. Remember, the target is not the hole. In putting, the target is an imaginary gate – or a mark on the green – 3 inches ahead of the ball. Aim at the gate, and if you hit through the gate with the proper power, the green will curve the ball into the hole.

You can't use a real gate while playing golf, but you should use a makeshift gate while practising.

On a practice green, set up a gate – put two coins on the green, 2 inches apart from each other – but don't select a target. Hit a lot of putts through the gate at different speeds. Focus your attention on trying to hit the ball straight off the head of the putter through the gate. You're not hitting to a hole, so your confidence will soar, because you'll be successful 100 per cent of the time. Notice that by hitting through the same gate with varying amounts of power, the ball curves and ends up in different places on the green. Though every putt started on the same line and went through the same gate, each one ended up in a completely different location. The speed made the putts stop in different locations. The main point of this exercise is to learn that the speed of a putt is the most important part of putting.

If you can hit through the gate every time, your technique is good enough to begin focusing on reading greens and hitting the ball with the correct amount of power to have the ball go in the hole.

When students do this drill, I often tell them, 'If the hole was the gate just ahead of your ball, what would be your chances of missing the putt?' Everybody gives the same answer: There's no chance of missing. Everybody, including the raw beginner, has total confidence that he or she can hit through a gate 3 inches ahead of the ball.

You'll know that you understand the concept of proper putting alignment when you start adjusting your clubface at address. You should notice that you have begun using your arms and hands to twist the putter face left or right to align it to the gate (imaginary or real). At this point in your putting education, don't think about your posture, except to ensure that you're balanced and comfortable.

The best way to determine if your clubhead is aligned correctly is to hit dozens of 6-inch putts into a hole. If you can make 25 6-inchers in a row, your alignment is fine.

Skill requirement: Your goal is to average four or fewer putts per hole for a nine-hole putting round on a practice green, incorporating a mix of short and long holes. You've completed Step 2 after having shot 36 or better per round for three nine-hole putting rounds.

FREE THINKERS

Throughout this book, I suggest concepts for you to think about while practising. In Step 2 of Putting, for example, I recommended that you concentrate on hitting through an imaginary gate 3 inches in front of your ball. It's unrealistic to mentally rehash every concept while playing; however, it is important while practising to remind yourself of key ideas until you've mastered them. You'll eventually reach a point where you can practise and play without thinking about specific concepts as much.

STEP 3: PRE-SHOT ROUTINE

Objectives: (1) To align your body and the putter to the target at address; (2) to develop a pre-shot routine.

Lesson: In Step 2, we were solely concerned with aligning the putter to the target at address. I said that your body could face any direction in which you feel comfortable. Indeed, it's possible to putt well while your body faces in any direction at address, but that doesn't mean it's easy. Here you'll learn to align your body properly with a putt.

Your body should be parallel to the target while putting. Standing a little open or a little closed is fine, but too much variation is likely to make it difficult, if not impossible, to align your putter squarely. There are two common signals for good body alignment. First, your belly button should point at the ball when you're ready to putt. Secondly, your toes should hit an imaginary line that runs basically parallel to the target.

Aligning your putter to the target, and then aligning your body to the target line, are elements of what is called the pre-shot routine. A pre-shot routine is what you do before hitting a shot to get yourself in the perfect position to make a good swing. A good analogy is preparing to fly a plane. Before taking off, a pilot goes through a long checklist to make sure the plane's mechanical systems are properly working. You need to be just as careful before hitting a golf shot as a pilot is before taking the controls of a plane. If the pilot forgets to put the flaps in the correct position, the plane could crash during take-off. This might seem like an extreme analogy, but if you're going to hit a good golf shot, you need to go through your personal swing checklist to get your body properly aligned.

Watch a professional tournament on TV, paying special attention to the players while they are putting. Watch them just before they putt. They usually survey the green to determine how hard to hit the putt and which way the ground will curve the ball as it rolls towards the target. Then, they approach the ball, walking to it from the side and a little behind. While approaching the ball, their eyes rock back and forth from the hole to their target and then to the ball. Sometimes Jack Nicklaus rocks his head ten or more times on a single putt. While lining up the putt, the pro is simultaneously aligning his body and his putter to the target.

At address, your body should be in a comfortable position, and your clubhead should face the target. No matter how you stand, the putter has to aim directly at the target 3 inches ahead of the ball. Making these adjustments before you putt should become instinctive, but it does take a little practice. When you're lining up a 12-foot putt in the last round of the US Open, you don't want to have to look at your hands and hips to make sure they're in the right position. You want to settle your body and the putter naturally into their correct positions.

MY PRE-SHOT ROUTINE
Everyone has a different pre-shot routine. Here's mine. You certainly don't need to copy it, but feel free to include the basic elements in developing your pre-shot routine.

1. Let's say I have a 20-foot putt. As I approach the green, I begin to survey its surface, determining the high and low points of the green. Remember, a putt will break towards the low point and away from the high point. What I am looking for here are the obvious contours on the green that'll affect how my ball rolls. Once on the green, I walk in a wide circle around the hole and my ball, studying the green's surface.
2. After gathering information for determining speed and distance, I stand 6 feet behind the ball and visualise exactly the direction I want to launch my ball. I pick out a spot of grass where I'd put my target gate. Then I slowly approach the ball, holding the putter in my right hand. I look back and forth, from the hole to the imaginary gate to the hole, as I walk to the ball. On reaching the ball, I begin adjusting my body to get my toe line and my putter pointed along the target line.
3. Still with only my right hand holding the club, I set the putter behind the ball, allowing the clubhead to rest lightly on the

turf. Now I put my left hand on the club, and adjust my grip to make it comfortable. Simultaneously, I adjust my stance and cock my head back and forth a few times, looking at the hole, the target and the ball, and I keep making minor adjustments until I am in perfect balance.

4. Then I take one last glance at the target and the hole, and then I hit the ball.

The total time for my routine, starting with the moment I begin approaching my ball, is about 20 seconds – much less time than it takes for me to describe it. Taking longer than that is not only a waste of time; it will throw off your rhythm and you'll have too much time in which you'll be prone to 'overthink' the putt. While putting, you have to trust your instincts.

A good putter always uses the same routine. Spend some time every day, at home or the course, practising your pre-shot putting routine. Don't actually hit any putts, though. Once you get into the address position, step away before swinging, and start over. Develop a routine that is your own.

Skill
requirement: Your goal is to average 3.5 or fewer putts per hole for an 18-hole putting round on a practice green, incorporating a mix of short and long holes. You've completed Step 3 after having shot 63 or better per round for three 18-hole putting rounds.

STEP 4: OWN YOUR STROKE

Objectives: (1) To understand proper ball location; and (2) to be able to explain your address position to a friend.

Lesson: In Step 3, I introduced body alignment and the pre-shot routine. Now I want to explain a few basic elements of ball position, because this concept is essential to assuring that you have proper alignment.

When putting, the ball should be an inch or two inside your left heel if you are right-handed. Feel free to vary this position if you find it's more comfortable to have the ball a little closer to the middle of your stance or closer to your left heel.

How far away should the ball be from your feet? There's no hard and fast rule, but, generally, your eyes should be directly above the ball at address. For most people, that means the ball will be about 12 inches from their feet. It's OK to stand very tall and have the ball close to your feet, like Raymond Floyd, or stand a little hunched over and have the ball a little farther from your feet, like Justin Leonard. Both players are good putters.

Go to a practice green with your putter. Hit lots of putts, varying the ball position. Hit putts with the ball as far towards the foot closest to the hole as you can and still make solid contact; as close to the foot that's farthest from the hole; and several positions in between your feet. Once you determine the most comfortable ball location, you've worked out the last element of your address position. Now you know how to align your body and the putter, and how to get into the proper position before putting.

In putting, it doesn't much matter how you grip the club. As long as the club feels comfortable, and as long as you make solid contact, hold the club however you like. There is no 'standard' grip that you should use. I've seen so many different grips used by LPGA and PGA Tour tournament winners, I can't remember all the wacky ways players hold their putters.

Two things all good putters have in common are: (1) they grip the club gently; and (2) they know their address positions and pre-shot routines so well that they can describe them to anybody. I want you to learn the details of your stroke. You should be able to describe how arched your back is at address; how wide your feet are; where the ball is relative to your body; whether your stroke is wristy or not; how many practice strokes you take; which hand you hold the putter with just before you step up to the ball.

I call this 'owning' your putting technique. It involves becoming intimately familiar with all aspects of the stroke, from how you read the greens to your pre-shot routine, to your address position and finally your stroke. It's difficult to putt well if you're changing positions from putt to putt or from round to round. Look at pictures of Jack Nicklaus on the green when he was 20 years old and when he was 60. He looks exactly the same.

If you own your stroke, you'll be less apt to want to change it after a bad putting day. If you really own your stroke, you'll have no problem brushing off a bad round, because your technique is solid and you know it. Nothing works 100 per cent of the time. Golfers are too quick to seek change after a bad shot or a bad round. My advice is to forget the bad rounds! If you putt badly twenty days in a row, then you might want to schedule a lesson.

Skill requirement:	Your goal is to average three or fewer putts per hole for an 18-hole putting round on a practice green, incorporating a mix of short and long holes. You've completed Step 4 after having shot 54 or better per round for three 18-hole putting rounds.

STEP 5: PRACTICE, PRACTICE, PRACTICE

Objective: To develop a balanced address position and a smooth putting stroke.

Lesson: A car with a standard transmission has a gearshift that you manually change. It's not too difficult to learn to drive a car with a standard transmission, but it takes some practice to learn to change gears smoothly. After manoeuvring the gearshift into a new position, one foot gently lets up on the clutch while the other foot gently presses down on the accelerator pedal. It's a matter of touch, and touch is a skill everybody can develop, but doing so takes practice.

The same is true with putting. By now you've learned the basics about putting, so the final element you need is a smooth, even and repeatable stroke. It's a stroke you know inside and out and can trust under all circumstances, whether you're playing for fun or for the Masters.

A stroke is smooth and even when the putter travels the same distance away from the ball as it does past the ball. Try making your backswing and follow-through like a pendulum, moving the club back away from the ball and then forwards straight through the ball. The speed and size of the stroke will determine the power. A big stroke that moves fast hits the ball a longer distance, and a short, slow swing will hit the ball a shorter distance. In all strokes, the putter should travel at approximately the same speed throughout the stroke.

If you closely analysed a great putting stroke, you'd find that it moves a shade quicker on the follow-through than the backswing. But that's a fine detail that you should not try to emulate. It will happen naturally if you putt smoothly and evenly. There shouldn't be any violent acceleration or deceleration during the stroke.

By now, you should have a good understanding of how to read greens. You should feel as if you can putt well. You won't make every putt, but you'll always feel confident that you have a chance. You should experiment with different putters, and make sure you like the one you have.

There's only one way to develop an efficient and consistent stroke: practice. How should you practise? Devote 20 minutes or longer to putting every time you visit the practice putting green. While you're going through this programme, I suggest you visit the putting green twice a week, though more often is better. If you can't get to a golf course, putt in your house or anywhere you can find a smooth surface.

You can fill your practice sessions with drills and playing games. I've provided five drills on the following pages, and you'll find putting games in Chapter 9. But please don't limit yourself to the drills and games I've provided. Create your own. Get drills from your friends. Do whatever is fun.

Skill   Your goal is to average 2.5 or fewer putts per hole
requirement: for an 18-hole putting round on a practice green,

incorporating a mix of short and long holes. You've completed Step 5 after having shot 45 or better per round for three 18-hole putting rounds.

MY FAVOURITE PUTTING DRILLS

1. SIX 10S
This drill gives you a way to divide an hour-long putting session into six 10-minute intervals. Here's what to do during each interval.

1. Use three balls. Hit putts, ranging from 1 to 3 feet in length, which are straight and uphill. Spend a few minutes at each of two different holes, varying the distances from putt to putt so you never hit two consecutive putts from the same spot. Don't hole out putts that you miss.
2. Use three balls. Hit putts, ranging from 3 to 6 feet, which are straight and uphill. Spend a few minutes at each of two different holes, varying the distances from putt to putt so you never hit two consecutive putts from the same spot. Don't hole out putts that you miss.
3. Use three balls. Hit the longest putts you can find on your practice green. Hit each ball until it goes into the hole.
4. Use three balls. Hit sets of 6-foot putts, doing each set from one of four different sides of the hole. Hit three putts from each spot, and then move to another spot. Imagine there's a circle around the hole, and the putting spots are noon, three o'clock, six o'clock and nine o'clock. Don't hole out putts that you miss. Keep circling the hole until 10 minutes have elapsed.
5. Repeat step 3. This drill teaches distance control, and you repeat the step because distance control is so important.
6. Play 18 holes on the practice green with one ball, holing out on every hole and keeping score.

2. STOP AND GO
Find a straight, 6-foot uphill putt on the practice green. Put three coins (or tees) in a line parallel to the target line, about 6

inches from the ball and on the opposite side of the ball from where you're standing. One coin should be adjacent to the ball; the second coin should be 8 inches towards the hole and the third coin should be 8 inches away from the hole. The row of coins should be parallel to your toe line.

During the stroke, stop the putter when it reaches the coin that's farthest from the target. Pause for a second, holding the putter at the endpoint of the backswing, and then continue the stroke. Repeat this action, swinging back and forth, holding the putter at the end of the backswing and then at the end of the follow-through in each stroke.

Do this five times without a ball, and then ten times with a ball, hitting the ball forwards. Do five sets, with 15 putts per set. You can do this at home or at the course.

At first, it'll probably be difficult to stop directly parallel to the coins on the backswing and follow-through. Most people will push the putter beyond the coins, which means they probably need to shorten the length of their strokes. In most cases, you can generate plenty of power with a stroke that's shorter than you think you'll need.

3. LOOK MUM, NO EYES!

Practise putting with your eyes closed on 6-footers, hitting from uphill and downhill lies. This will be a great help in learning the difference in feel between a good stroke – which is smooth and rhythmic – and a bad stroke, which is choppy.

This is my favourite drill because, with your eyes closed, you can focus solely on the smoothness of your stroke, and you can be in tune with what your body must feel like to make a smooth and rhythmic stroke. I like this drill so much that I often play entire rounds putting with my eyes closed.

4. HOLD THE FINISH

On a practice green, play from hole to hole, making sure to hold your follow-through position until the ball stops rolling on every single putt. That means you'll hold your putter in the air and out in front of your feet. Don't try to push the club farther than you normally do. Just hold it where it finishes in a regular stroke. Holding the finish is another way to help develop good feel for a smooth and even stroke.

5. AROUND THE WORLD
On a practice green, place about 15 balls around a hole so that the balls create a circle. Each ball should be approximately 5 feet from the hole. Hit each ball to the hole. If you miss, don't hit the ball again. Just knock it out of the circle, and move on to the next ball in the circle.

6. LESS-THAN-FULL SWING

THE MOTION USED FOR MORE THAN HALF THE SHOTS IN GOLF, AND THE FOUNDATION OF THE FULL SWING

The moral of golf – if we can say there is a moral to any sport – is that every shot counts the same, whether it's a 5-yard chip or a 337-yard drive. Tiger Woods is one of the longest hitters on the Tour, averaging nearly 300 yards per drive. But Tiger has always understood golf better than most.

When Tiger was six years old, he had no trouble beating kids who were seven or eight years older than he was. Back then, he couldn't drive the ball nearly as far as the older kids, but it didn't matter. On an average length par 4, Tiger would take three shots to reach the green, and then he would usually take no more than three short shots – a combination of chips and putts – to hole out. Meanwhile, his opponents – the kids who were more than twice his age and double his size – would hit much wilder shots, blasting balls into the woods, duffing chips and yipping putts. So despite his physical disadvantage, Tiger's accuracy and composure allowed him to usually shoot the lowest score. Who do you think went home smiling most often?

Every golfer wants to hit huge drives, hole putts and shoot low scores. Doing that is possible, but in order to do that you need to have good control in all aspects of the game. This chapter focuses on learning how to master the less-than-full swing technique – a small version of the full swing.

At least 60 per cent of the shots in golf are short – from 1-foot putts to 75-yard approaches – and these short shots usually require hitting with less power than full shots. To reduce power in the swing, you don't just take a gentler swing; you also take a smaller swing, one that is less than full.

Few golfers ever truly realise how important the less-than-full swing action is in golf. As a result, golfers rarely practise this important part of the game. But people who dedicate significant time to the less-than-full swing are usually the best players.

I suggest you keep track of every shot for a few rounds, noting whether the shot is a full swing, a less-than-full swing or a putt, and the distance of the shot. You'll be surprised at how many shots are within 75 yards of the green, and the exercise should convince you to devote at least half, if not more, of your practice time to the short game.

Here's another reason to emphasise practising less-than-full swing techniques. Most pros hit almost every shot – drives, chips and everything in between – with a less-than-full swing motion. If you think Phil Mickelson and Tiger Woods hit long balls in tournaments, you should see how far they hit when they use full power. In competition, tour pros hit most shots at 80 to 90 per cent of capacity. Tour players rarely swing as hard and as big as they are capable of doing on more than a few shots in each round. Swinging like this, with a compact and shortened version of the full swing, pros can hit a single club many different distances. That's an advanced skill, but it's a necessary skill for anybody who wants to play good golf, and it's a skill that every golfer *can* learn.

If you can hit each individual club only one distance, then you will encounter significant distance ranges for which you don't have a proper shot. Say you can hit, with an average swing, a 7-iron 130 yards and a 6-iron 145 yards, and your ball is 137 yards from the hole. If you don't know how to hit your 6-iron with a less-than-full swing, you won't have a club to hit to the green with. Your only option will be to swing extra hard with a 7-iron, and overswinging will almost always cause you to be out of balance and diminish your chances of hitting a good shot.

You can't be a great golfer if you take a full swing on every shot. That's why long-driving champions like Jason Zuback, a four-time winner of the National Long Drive competition, rarely have success as tour professionals. The golfers who always swing full-bore have great difficulty controlling the speed of the club and therefore can't control the distances they hit. Indeed, Zuback, knowing his limitations, has never even tried to qualify for the PGA Tour, despite the fact that his average drive exceeds

350 yards (in normal conditions) and it's not uncommon for him to uncork 400-yarders.

The lone former Long Drive champion on the PGA Tour is Dennis Paulson. But Paulson struggled as a tour professional for over a decade because he refused to stop swinging for the fences, failing eight times at the PGA Tour Qualifying tournament, beginning in 1985. He finally earned a Tour card for the 1994 season, but by 1996 he had lost his card and was back where he'd started – on the mini-tours. It was then that Paulson began to rein in his massive swing and focus more intently on employing a less-than-full swing motion more often. Paulson again qualified for the Tour in 1999, and the following year he won his first Tour event, the Buick Classic.

Here are the five steps for the less-than-full swing.

STEP 1: The grip and broomstick basics
STEP 2: The slap shot
STEP 3: How to hit different distances
STEP 4: A balanced weight transfer
STEP 5: Know your swing

STEP 1: THE GRIP AND BROOMSTICK BASICS

Objectives: (1) To learn a simple grip; and (2) to swing in a pendulum motion while brushing the ground with a lofted club.

Lesson: The best place to work on Step 1 is a practice tee with lots of grass. You'll need a broom – yes, a broom! – a wedge and a few buckets of practice balls.

I rarely begin a lesson by discussing the details of the grip, ball position or alignment. A golfer may naturally have a good grip and proper alignment, so I don't want to provide information that could confuse him or her or change something that's already good. It's important in golf to let assumptions be positive rather than negative. I've seen many beginners who have no golf knowledge and have had no previous instruction swing with excellent technique.

We're going to focus on just one important skill in Step 1: brushing, or sweeping, the club. You want to take a very little swing in which the broom will brush across the top of the ground, its bottom edge grazing the grass as it sweeps through the impact zone. The impact zone is the area that stretches 2 feet in either direction of the ball to and from the hole.

On the practice tee, grip the middle of the broom's handle with both hands. Use whatever grip feels comfortable. What comes naturally is perfectly acceptable right now. You can make modifications to your grip later – if they are necessary.

I understand that every practice range won't have a broom to use to train your swing motion. If your range doesn't have a broom, simply bring a broom to the range or do these broom-brushing drills at home before going to the course.

Stick the broom's handle under your left armpit, if you're right-handed. The end of the broomstick should stick out behind your left shoulder, and the bristles should gently touch the ground where the golf ball would be.

Now, quickly sweep the broom back and forth a few times, holding the broom handle under your armpit by firmly squeezing your left arm against your side. Your wrists should be relaxed and loose, naturally bending as the broom sweeps back and forth moving through the impact zone. The length of the sweeping motion should be about 4 feet in each direction.

This sweeping motion is the same motion you will soon use to hit balls with a club. It's a good idea to sweep back and forth with the broom for a couple of minutes every day while you are learning the game. Some expert players and teachers also practise the sweeping motion with a broom to keep their swing grooved, or to relearn the proper motion when their swing is out of whack.

Once you've practised the sweeping motion and are comfort-able with it, the next step is to learn about a good golf grip. Take a 9-iron or a wedge, which, you might be surprised to learn, are the heaviest clubs in golf (the driver is the lightest). Grip the club with both hands, employing the same grip you used on the broom. Be sure your hands are near each other and that you hold the club firmly enough so that it won't fly out of your hands while swinging.

Now you're going to modify your grip, if it is not already correct. Here is the proper way to grip the golf club.

Your left hand goes on the upper end of the grip, towards the grip's butt (or end), if you're a right-handed player. Your right hand should sit on the grip just below the left hand. The palm of your right hand covers your left thumb, and the index finger of your left hand and the little finger of your right hand either interlock or overlap. Both interlock and overlap grips are good. (Tiger and Jack Nicklaus use an interlock, while Ben Hogan used an overlap. My preference is the interlock.) The space between your right thumb and your right index finger forms a V. The hands should be close together, forming a single unit.

LITTLE SHOTS MAKE BIG IMPRESSIONS

While the public drools over Tiger's long shots, not as much is said about his short game. But I've always been most impressed by the mind-boggling little shots he's been hitting since I met him.

Even as a four-year-old, Tiger's short game and finesse shots were the most impressive parts of his repertoire. As a kid, he could hit high floaters and low screamers with his 7-iron, and a low running pitch and a soft lob with his wedge. Tiger seemed to have all these shots down perfectly, and his ability to hit them successfully in competition meant that he was miles ahead of the players who could hit the ball twice as far.

During a round Tiger and I played at the Navy Base Golf Course when he was ten, Tiger had a 20-yard pitch from soggy dirt and he had to carry a bunker to hit the green. It was a nasty lie. I would have been happy just to clear the bunker, although a skull or chunk would have been more likely.

Tiger confidently approached the ball, looking like Ted Williams stepping up to the plate. His eyes were intently focused on the target. Fear wasn't a factor. He took a huge swing, nipped the ball and flopped it high in the air. It sailed over the bunker, on to the green and rolled a few feet before stopping 2 feet from the hole.

SWING SIZE

Get into a balanced and comfortable stance. Again, if your address position feels comfortable, it's OK for now, and maybe forever. Without a ball, sweep the club back and forth just like you did with the broom. The clubhead should graze the top of the grass. Don't try to do anything special with the swing or your body, like keeping your arms firm or breaking your wrists at a certain point. Do what comes naturally.

How big should you swing? To gauge the size of a swing, imagine you're standing in front of a clock that's a little taller than you are, with your back facing the clock. You measure the size of your swing by matching the position of your hands to the hours on the clock. If you want to swing from eight o'clock to two o'clock, your hands will stop at eight o'clock on the backswing and at two o'clock on the follow-through.

Now, take several swings going back to seven o'clock and through to five o'clock. This is a very small swing, the goal being to brush the ground with the leading edge of the club. Swing back and forth without stopping, keeping your eyes focused on the spot where the ball would be.

It'll be difficult to take such small swings because the tendency is to take the club back and through farther than I've suggested. But you must force yourself to make the small swings by focusing on controlling the size of your swing.

After you feel comfortable with this little swing, or sweeping motion, you're ready to hit some balls. Use the same small swing, with your lone thought being to generate a rhythmic and compact sweeping motion. Don't think about making contact with the ball. If you swing correctly, the club will hit the ball.

If you hit a few poor shots, don't worry. You should not yet be concerned where the ball is going. You're just learning to sweep the club. Also, at the end of the follow-through, you want to hold the club out in front of your body. You do this because it's the natural position to swing to if you have made a good swing motion. Holding the club is also the best way to gauge if you are in perfect balance. If, in fact, you are well balanced at the end of the swing, somebody should be able to nudge you on the shoulder and you won't wobble.

Skill *requirement:* Select a target 10 yards away. You can aim at anything – a flag on a green, a yardage marker or patch of discoloured grass, or a stick in the ground. Hit very small shots with a wedge or 9-iron, swinging back to seven o'clock and through to five o'clock and holding your finish position until the ball stops rolling. In a good shot, the club will solidly hit the ball, launching it into the air so it flies about 10 yards, rolls a little and stops within 10 feet of the target. The goal is to hit seven out of ten shots successfully within 10 feet of the target. After doing that on each of two different days, you should begin Step 2.

STEP 2: THE SLAP SHOT

Objectives: (1) To develop the proper release, or wrist action, throughout the swing; and (2) to learn the proper ball position at address.

Lesson: In Step 2, you're going to learn the proper ball position. Ball position is where your golf ball is located on the ground relative to your body. The ball's location is the same for all shots. That location is one clubhead inside the target-side foot (the left foot for a right-handed player). The right foot's location depends on the size of the swing; the bigger the swing, the wider the stance. Also, the ball should sit a distance from your body in which you don't have to reach or feel cramped.

Next, we're going to learn about wrist action, often called the release. You're going to add wrist action to your less-than-full swing and lengthen the basic sweeping motion that you learned in Step 1. The wrist action will provide additional swing speed and power. You're also going to learn what it feels like to release the clubhead as it's travelling through the impact zone.

Here's an exercise that will help you understand wrist action. Stand tall and raise your right hand to breast height and put it 8 inches in front of your body, keeping the elbow close to your side. Quickly cock the hand ten times back and forth, like a windscreen wiper. Then put the right hand down and raise your left hand. Quickly cock this hand back and forth ten times. Now put your hands together in front of your chest, pretending to grip an imaginary club as if the clubhead points at the sky. Cock your hands back and forth, bending mostly at the wrists. The wrists and elbows should freely bend while you maintain constant grip pressure throughout the cocking motion.

You should be holding the club with your fingers, allowing your wrists and elbows to bend. During the swing, golfers tend to let go of the club with their fingers, and they don't allow their wrists and elbows to bend.

Go to the chipping green or the practice range with a wedge and a bucket of balls. In Step 1 you hit shots that flew 10 yards. Now you're going to try to hit the ball 50 yards with a swing that goes back to nine o'clock and through to three o'clock. Address the ball the way you did in Step 1, focusing primarily on being balanced and comfortable. You don't want to reach for the ball or feel cramped over it.

BACKSWING BASICS

Address a ball, and begin a swing by turning your shoulders away from the target, and letting your wrist cock, sweep the club back from the ball and up towards the sky. You should allow your wrists to bend smoothly as your hands move back and up towards nine o'clock. Keep turning and bending your wrists until the clubhead and the shaft are pointing up to the sky. At this point, your hands should be at nine o'clock and approximately over your right foot.

Until you feel comfortable with this swing motion, follow the club with your eyes as you swing it back. Doing that will help you learn what happens to your body and the club during the swing, and it's usually easier to do something if you understand how it works.

Once the club reaches nine o'clock, and the shaft is pointed at the sky, start the downswing by turning your torso back towards the target and sweeping the club down towards the impact zone and stop the club just before it hits the ball. Repeat this back-and-forth, half-swing motion several times in succession. Concentrate on feeling the club move away from the ball and then up towards the sky as you add a little bit of wrist cock. Remember, your wrists and elbows bend and the fingers hold the club. When you stop the club just before the ball, you should sense that if you had continued the swing, there would have been a powerful hit to the ball.

BEWARE OF INFORMATION OVERLOAD

TIME OUT!
Let's take a breather if these instructions are getting too technical. I don't want you to get bogged down by information and start swinging like a robot. I'm giving detailed descriptions because I want to answer any questions you might ask if we were working together in person. But the truth is, I teach many players concepts in Step 2 without ever having to give them as much information as I do in this book. Swinging a golf club is a natural movement and most people do it correctly without thinking about all these details.

LIGHTS, CAMERA, ACTION

As a child, Tiger appeared on dozens of television shows, many of them news and sports programmes in the Los Angeles area. I was often present at the tapings. One of my favourite tapings occurred when Tiger was seven years old and he was featured on Two on the Town, *a TV magazine show produced by CBS's Channel 2 in Los Angeles.*

The segment was taped at Heartwell Golf Park in Long Beach. The station filmed Tiger playing nine holes with his

*father and me. On the fifth hole, a 100-yard par 3, Tiger
missed the green by a few yards and was 40 feet from the
flagstick. He had a pretty good lie, his orange ball sitting in light
rough. The cameraman was standing right over Tiger, and I
thought he was too close and would disturb Tiger's
concentration. Tiger's dad, Earl, was standing by the green, too.*

*Tiger wasn't fazed. He was in his zone – the same zone he
gets into today – and went about his business as if he were the
only person on the course. Tiger studied the shot for a moment,
analysing his lie and the turf between his ball and the hole. He
then took his cut-down pitching wedge out of his bag. The club,
made by Confidence Golf Company, was one of his favourites.*

*Tiger hit a little chip and run. He stayed in perfect balance
throughout the swing. He made a complete turn, back and
through, his wrists calmly bending the club back to eight o'clock
and through to four o'clock. The ball flew 10 feet in the air,
landed on the green and rolled 30 feet directly into the centre of
the hole. Earl was so excited that he burst into laughter. I
wasn't surprised, though, because Tiger chipped in a lot.*

After developing your backswing, you're going to learn to
make the same motion on the follow-through. In that, your left
wrist starts to bend as the club travels through the impact zone.
In the backswing, your right wrist did most of the bending, but
in the follow-through the left wrist does a majority of the
bending.

Swing your wedge or 9-iron back to nine o'clock and through
to three o'clock several times in succession, until you smoothly
brush the ground on a series of swings. This action should feel
much more powerful than the Step 1 sweeping motion. You are
beginning to feel the full release of the club at impact, and that
release delivers the power to the ball. My favourite term for this
proper release is 'slapping the ball with the clubface'. In most
lessons, I repeatedly tell the student to 'slap the ball'. New
students tend to hold back and do not allow the wrists to bend,
and they don't slap hard enough. It's almost impossible to have
too much wrist bend or to slap too hard.

OILY WRISTS

Don't worry about the path along which your club travels during the little swings. Just focus on taking the club back – in this step to nine o'clock and through to three o'clock – and on maintaining perfect balance and slapping the ball.

Your wrists can become too stiff if you don't allow them to bend naturally. It's important to maintain constant grip pressure and allow your wrists and elbows to bend. I've already made this point several times in this chapter, but I can't emphasise it enough. In a 30-minute lesson, I might tell a student ten or fifteen times to let his wrists and elbows bend.

When I'm working with someone who has trouble bending his or her wrists and elbows, I pretend that I am holding an oilcan in my right hand. I point the imaginary can at the student's wrists while he swings, and with my mouth I make the clicking sound that a small oilcan makes when dispensing oil. The goal is to make students feel like their wrists are fully lubricated and moving freely during the swing. Control doesn't come from stiff wrists. It comes from perfect balance and relaxed wrists.

With your 9-iron or wedge, slap a bunch of shots, hitting the ball 50 yards. Each time you swing, follow through and hold your balance at the finish, with the clubhead pointed to the sky and your hands at three o'clock. Hold this position until the ball stops rolling. You hold your finish to evaluate your balance. If you were in balance during the swing, you'll be in balance at the finish. If you were off balance during the swing, you won't be in balance at the finish.

If you top or miss a ball, that's OK. Forget it and move on. Even tour players occasionally top shots. Never dwell on bad shots. After a good shot, however, I want you to think about what it felt like so you'll remember the feeling. Tell a friend what a good shot feels like, or, if you're alone, pause after each good shot and think why it was good. I suggest you write these ideas in a golf notebook.

Here are three key elements of my balanced less-than-full swing motion.

1. In the backswing, I feel a little shoulder turn. My wrists feel oily, very loose and free, and I can sense the club breaking up towards the sky as it moves backwards.
2. At the beginning of the downswing, I feel my torso turning back towards the target at the same time as my club releases into the ball.
3. Just after hitting the ball, I feel the clubhead travelling around my torso and up a little. I finish with the clubhead facing the sky, and I'm in perfect balance on top of my left foot, with my elbows fully bent.

Skill requirement: Hit at least ten buckets of practice balls using only a short swing, with the largest motion going back to nine o'clock and through to three o'clock. After at least ten buckets, take one more bucket and count your good shots. In a good shot, you cleanly nip the ball and it flies up to 50 yards and stops within 30 feet of the target. You should be in perfect balance after each shot. After you hit 30 out of 50 balls well on each of two different days, you've completed Step 2.

STEP 3: HOW TO HIT DIFFERENT DISTANCES

Objectives: (1) To hit short shots with every club in the bag; (2) to learn how different clubs hit balls different distances; and (3) to understand that each club can produce a variety of distances.

Lesson: In Step 3, you'll use the less-than-full swing motion that you learned in Step 2 to hit shots with every club in your bag. You'll also learn how to control the ball's distance.

Changing clubs is one way to make the ball go different distances. A sand wedge makes the ball go shorter than a 5-iron does because the sand wedge has more loft and a shorter shaft than a 5-iron. Because the wedge is short and the 5-iron is longer, the 5-iron clubhead travels at a faster speed with the same amount of effort in the swing. Combine that extra speed with less loft, and the 5-iron makes the ball go farther than the wedge.

As you change from club to club, the shaft length and clubhead loft of each club will determine the distance the ball will travel.

LOFT AND LENGTH
Length is determined by the size of the shaft, which is measured from the top of the grip to the bottom of the sole of the clubhead. Loft, in basic terms, is the backward slant of the clubhead in relation to the ground when the club lies flat on the ground. Among a set of irons, a wedge has the most loft and a 1-iron has the least loft. Among woods, a driver has the least loft, a 2-wood the second-least loft, and down the line. Putters have very little loft.

There are general guidelines for loft and length in relation to specific clubs. But not all clubs have the same loft and length. For example, a 6-iron from one company could have 36 degrees of loft and a 37-inch shaft while another company's 6-iron could have 33 degrees of loft and a 37.5-inch shaft.

The loft and shaft length variations among companies are usually small, and shouldn't have much – if any – effect on how you play the game. But as you become a more skilled player, loft might become more important to you. If that happens, the only way to learn what lofts you like with specific clubs is through experimentation.

The chart overleaf shows the standard loft and length for each club.

You can also hit different distances by varying the swing size. For example, you could use a 5-iron with a full swing to hit a ball the same distance you'd achieve by hitting a 4-iron with a slightly smaller swing. Both shots travel the same distance, but you use different swings. You need to have the ability to hit both of these shots because to play good golf you need to control the distance the ball goes. And to do that, you have to know how to adjust your club selection and modify the size of your swing.

CLUB	LOFT	LENGTH	CLUB	LOFT	LENGTH
Driver	10°	44.5"	1-iron	16°	40.0"
3-wood	16°	43.5"	2-iron	20°	39.0"
5-wood	20°	42.5"	3-iron	24°	38.5"
7-wood	24°	41.5"	4-iron	28°	38.0"
			5-iron	32°	37.5"
			6-iron	36°	37.0"
			7-iron	40°	36.5"
			8-iron	44°	36.0"
			9-iron	48°	35.5"
			Pitching wedge	52°	35.5"
			Sand wedge	56°	35.5"
			Lob wedge	60°	35.5"
			Putter	4°	35.5"

ONE-CLUB WONDER

It's possible to create so many different distances with a single club that some people play golf with just one club. Seve Ballesteros learned to play golf using only a cut-down 3-iron, and he could make the ball do almost anything with that club. But Seve didn't learn with one club because he wanted to. It was the only club he had.

Now you're going to use the brushing and slapping techniques you've already learned, applying those techniques to different clubs to make the ball fly different distances.

On the practice range, use a small, less-than-full swing motion to hit shots with all of your clubs, from the sand wedge to the driver. The swing should go back to nine o'clock and through to three o'clock. Hold the finish after every shot, making sure that the club is pointing at the sky. Watch the ball travel, observing how much it flies and then rolls. This information will be vital once you start to play, because you need to be able to determine which club to use on each shot.

TRAJECTORY

Go to a practice green where you can chip and bring all your clubs. Prepare to hit shots standing within 10 feet of the green. You're going to hit to different targets depending on which club you use. The balls should fly in the air a little, land on the green – not too close to the edge – and roll to the target. You're just focusing on making solid contact and getting the ball to fly onto the green.

You should notice that you could use every club – from the wedge through to the driver – to hit chip shots and get the ball close to the hole with a minimum amount of effort. By changing clubs, you can control how far the ball rolls after it lands. For example, a 5-iron shot will roll a lot farther than a pitching wedge shot after the ball hits the green. The loft of the golf club is the reason that this happens. A 5-iron has less loft than a pitching wedge. Thus, a ball hit with a 5-iron has more 'forward energy' than 'up energy' and therefore will roll farther after it lands than if hit with a pitching wedge.

By changing clubs around the green, you can vary how far the ball rolls. Hit shots with all your clubs, noticing how high the ball flies and then how far it rolls after landing. You need these different shots to deal with the variety of situations you'll encounter around the greens when you play golf. You could chip with one club all the time, but doing that limits your shot-making capability.

Recently, tour pros have begun using metal woods to hit some delicate chips from the edge of the green, in part because Tiger has used the shot with great success. Using a metal wood from within a few feet of the green can be advantageous because the clubhead has a big sole and not much loft, and the clubhead easily glides through the grass. A ball hit with a wood from around the green will roll a long way, because woods have less loft than the irons that you would normally chip with.

While you're practising around the green, experiment hitting from different lengths of grass. Hit from the fringe and from the thickest grass you can find within a few feet of a green. Place your balls on top of the grass, and also gently step on them so they are buried as deep as possible. You're going to face many different situations on the course, so you might as well practise from them.

It's OK to try your 3-wood and driver out of long grass. See what it feels like and how the ball reacts. You might learn something nobody else knows and develop a successful shot that'll help you win a tournament. You might learn to hit a shot like Phil Mickelson's famous flop, which, with a 60-degree wedge and from an uphill lie, he can hit up over his head and backwards – yes, *backwards*!

Skill
requirement: Hit four shots with each club in your bag from within 10 feet of the green. Two of the four shots with each club must stop within 10 feet of the pin. Do this requirement in two different sessions, hitting from a different position in each session.

STEP 4: A BALANCED WEIGHT TRANSFER

Objectives: (1) To learn a proper weight transfer; and 2) to stay in perfect balance while hitting less-than-full swing shots.

Lesson: In Step 4, you want to achieve a basic level of consistency with distance and accuracy. First, we'll concentrate on balance, the foundation of all good shots. I like to say, 'Balance equals control.' Good balance is often the cause of the correct swing action, whereas bad balance cannot support a proper swing motion. Look to balance, not club positions, to find your control. After hitting a poor shot, many golfers immediately move the club back to a particular point in the swing, trying to analyse why the club didn't perform the way they thought it should. Golfers who do this are looking in the wrong place for the cause of their problem. They're studying the result – the bad swing position – when they should be analysing the cause – poor balance.

To stay in balance throughout the swing, you need to stay on top of your feet. Every swing, regardless of its size, requires some weight transfer. This weight transfer has to be made in balance, and to ensure that you're in balance, you must be over your feet. This rule applies to all golf shots, whether they are tiny pitches or bombs-away tee shots. This concept is similar to walking. We walk in balance whether we make little steps or run on a track. The size of the motion varies, but the balance doesn't.

The size of your weight transfer, or motion, determines the power of your shot. A small motion provides small power, and bigger motions provide bigger power.

At address, your weight should be evenly distributed between both feet. During the backswing, you rotate your torso horizontally and away from the target – and thus transfer the weight so that at the end of the backswing your weight should be primarily over the foot that is farthest from the target. On the follow-through, you rotate back towards the target, and in so doing transfer your weight through the impact zone, moving the club into the ball. After impact, your torso and the club continue to rotate forwards, towards the target, so that at the end of the swing your weight rests on top of your left foot.

I have a weight-transfer rule, which says that whatever weight you transfer back to the right foot is the same amount of weight you transfer to the left foot during the follow-through, if you are right-handed. If you transfer lots of weight during the back-swing and just a little weight in the follow-through, you'll almost certainly be off balance. An even weight transfer should produce good balance.

I like to compare golf's weight transfer to throwing a baseball. When you wind up to throw a ball, you first transfer your weight on to your back foot. At that point, your body is loaded with power. Try throwing a ball, or hitting a golf shot, with no weight transfer. The throw, or golf shot, will not go very far.

Some teachers break the weight transfer down into percentages. They recommend turning back so you have a specific percentage of weight over the right foot at the end of the backswing, and then turning through the ball so you have a certain percentage of your weight over the left foot at the end of the follow-through. Trying to replicate exact percentages is too difficult, because it steers your mind away from what's important: making a complete and balanced turn. It's much more useful to focus on letting your instincts tell you how much to transfer, depending on the power of the shot.

Here are some signs to look for to identify good balance at the end of the follow-through on the less-than-full swing shot we're practising, and on all other less-than-full swing and full-swing shots.

1. You're comfortably standing tall and looking at your target.
2. Your wrists and elbows are soft and bent.
3. You're holding the club with even grip pressure.

Now go to the range and use a wedge or lofted iron. Hit a bunch of pitches, swinging between ten o'clock and two o'clock.

Concentrate solely on (1) making a proper weight transfer, (2) slapping the ball and (3) staying in perfect balance during and after the swing. Don't think about mechanics – things like grip, posture and positioning of your feet. Trust that good balance will provide control and accuracy.

Students often hit the ball too far in Step 4. It's tempting to hit too long, because by now you're developing a good feel for the swing and making solid contact.

OOPS IS OKAY

You're going to hit some poor shots while practising and playing. Just laugh them off. They're part of the game. In 1964, Jack Nicklaus shanked an 8-iron on the par 3 twelfth hole in the Masters while playing with Arnold Palmer. None other than Bobby Jones and Clifford Roberts, the cofounders of both the Masters and Augusta National Golf Club, were in the gallery watching. 'It was a very pretty shank,' says Nicklaus. 'One of the best I ever hit. I usually don't remember bad shots, but I couldn't forget that one.'

If Jack Nicklaus can laugh off a terrible shot, so can you.

WHY RIGHT?

If you're hitting behind the ball, or the ball is going too far right – the cause is one of three things: (1) you're out of balance; (2) you're dropping or lowering your right shoulder during the swing, usually in an effort to get the clubhead under the ball. In a correct downswing, your torso, which includes your shoulders, should naturally rotate from right to left, or horizontally, not up and down. Keep your shoulders fairly level throughout the swing; or (3) you have stiff wrists and thus are leaving the clubface open at impact, which causes the ball to go right.

PARALYSIS BY ANALYSIS

Too often, golfers try to do a hundred different things in their swing. They think about cocking their head back just before beginning the swing, keeping their hands supple and holding their hands away from their body during the swing. The list goes on. Alone, each one of those moves is good. But trying to do them all simultaneously is impossible, because your mind will be so crowded with information that you'll probably forget how to swing the club smoothly and powerfully. This is called paralysis by analysis.

Skill *requirement*:	On the practice tee, swing back to ten o'clock and through to two o'clock. Hit ten shots with a wedge, ten with a 5-iron and ten with a fairway wood. Pick a different target for each club. Regardless of the distance you hit with a ten-to-two swing, five of ten shots with each club should be hit with solid contact and in good balance, and the ball should stop close to your target. Do that successfully in two different sessions, and you have completed Step 4.

STEP 5: KNOW YOUR SWING

Objective:	To be completely familiar with your less-than-full swing motion.
Lesson:	You're going to learn a few more intricacies about the swing. You're going to practise shots with the same size swing you used in Step 4, back to ten o'clock and through to two o'clock.

Turn and slap the ball through impact, keeping your hands and the club moving forwards and around until the hands reach two o'clock; the club should point up to the sky and slightly away from the target at the end of the swing. Your left wrist will be fully bent; you'll have even grip pressure; and you'll be in perfect balance facing the target. Your hands should be well out in front of your body and slightly to the left of it. Your weight, as in Step 4, will be on top of your left foot.

Your right heel has been pulled up off the ground a little, but it should not be totally rolled over. The momentum of your follow-through will naturally pull your right heel off the ground. You shouldn't move the right heel on purpose, but it should move as the result of a proper turn and weight transfer.

I suggest swinging back to ten and through to two on the driving range with a pitching wedge. Try hitting the ball to a specific target that's comfortable to reach. Sometimes you'll hit the ball much farther than at other times. That's good, and the long shots are the result of an efficient swing.

Continue to hold the club at the finish position after each shot and think about what happened during the swing. What did your rhythm and balance feel like? Did you make a good turn and slap motion? Did you allow your wrists and elbows to bend? If you hit a bad shot, still hold your position, but move your body to the position it should have been in if you had swung in perfect balance. This will help you learn what you should be doing, and you'll get to a good finish more frequently. Remember, motion is power, balance is control.

The biggest problem you'll have swinging from ten to two is that you'll instinctively swing bigger, probably back to twelve o'clock and through to twelve o'clock. Continually check your backswing and follow-through, looking only to see that your hands don't pass ten o'clock on the backswing and two o'clock on the follow-through.

While teaching this segment of the less-than-full swing, I often stand right next to the student and repeat my mantra, 'Turn and slap, turn and slap, turn and slap.' If you don't turn, the ball will go right – and if you don't slap, the ball will have no power. If you swing out of balance, you lose all control, and the ball could go anywhere.

You're going to start hitting lots of good shots at this point, and you'll be tempted to swing faster and hit it harder. But you shouldn't. Stay relaxed, and keep the swing between ten and two with perfect balance. This isn't a full-power swing. If I were watching you practise, you should be able to tell me, with no hesitation, that you're not swinging with full power. When I work with low-handicap players on this drill, I often have to ask them continually to swing smaller and gentler. You're learning a less-than-full power motion that hits the ball shorter distances.

Skill requirement: Hit hundreds of practice balls with the ten-o'clock-to-two-o'clock swing to develop your rhythm and balance for an effective less-than-full swing. The goal is to get in a groove and know your swing.

On two different days, solidly hit 30 out of 50 shots, finishing in perfect balance on each of the good shots. Use three different clubs – a wedge, a mid-iron and a wood. The shots don't have to be perfect; they just have to be solid, and you must finish in good balance. After doing this, you've completed Step 5.

7. THE FULL SWING
BALANCE IS CONTROL, MOTION IS POWER

There's no substitute for distance. No matter how far a golfer hits the ball, he or she should always strive to hit it farther. How far should you hit the golf ball? Long is good, longer is better and super-long is the best.

Of course, the short game is important, but don't underestimate the significance of the long game. The case of PGA Tour player Loren Roberts is telling. Loren is one of the best golfers on the planet; he putts like a magician, he has a rhythmic swing that produces solid contact almost all the time and he's got an unflappable mentality. Why, then, had Loren won only seven Tour events in two decades, at the end of 2001? Distance was a big reason.

Loren is one of the shortest hitters on the Tour, averaging around 260 yards per drive, nearly *20 yards less* than the average driving distance and 40 yards less than the longest hitters. Loren's shortness puts him at a huge disadvantage before he even tees off. He has to play perfect golf just to be in contention, because he hits so many long-iron and fairway-wood approaches when his competitors hit mid- to short-irons.

Golf, like so many other sports, is very much a power game. The world's best heavyweight boxer is always going to beat the world's best lightweight boxer, even if both fighters have equal boxing skill. No matter the sport, if two players have comparable ability but one is significantly stronger than the other, the stronger competitor will usually win. So in golf, you need to start your full-swing development by striving to develop as big a power base as possible.

A power base is a golfer's ability to generate clubhead speed, much like the horsepower in a car engine determines the power – and ultimately the speed – that a vehicle can generate. Clubhead speed is determined by the size of your motion – how far back and how far through you swing – and by how fast you swing. A fast swing with a big range of motion yields a big power base. It's essential to develop a big power base early in your golf career because once you get used to using a particular swing, it's hard to change that swing.

MAKE THE BIG DOG EAT

1. How do you maximise distance? (a) Swing with a full range of motion, making a complete weight transfer back during the backswing and through, towards the target, during the follow-through. (b) Stay in perfect balance throughout the swing.

   You don't have to try to swing extra hard to hit the ball far. You should always try to whack the ball, but overswinging is never good. Perhaps you've heard the saying, 'Swing nice and easy.' Golfers often believe that swinging easy will help them keep their swings in control, and consequently hit good shots. Wrong! Swinging easy never helped anybody play better golf. A golfer who swings easy usually does so because it's the only way he or she can hit the ball decently with a bad swing.

2. How hard should you swing? As a general rule, always swing as hard as you can without losing your balance. That goes for all shots except putts and other areas of the short game. As long as you are in balance while hitting a golf ball, you will have control over the ball. Remember this principle of golf: 'Balance is control, motion is power.'

TIGER HAS NEVER LIKED LOSING

Tiger and I loved competing against each other. We usually played stroke-play matches and had a lot of good-natured trash talk. I enjoyed beating him because he was so good and so competitive.

He was much more skilled than I was, but he couldn't hit the ball far enough to shoot low scores from the back tees. He was always looking to gain the upper hand, even when we weren't on the course. On a drive home after we had played a round together when he was only six years old, I reminded him that I'd beaten him that day and that I owned him. Tiger responded by saying, 'You may own me, Rudy, but the police own you.'

Let me explain. I used to drive a white Porsche 911 Targa. I loved driving fast and got several speeding tickets. Tiger has always been able to find a way to win, and back then he was clever enough to use my speeding-ticket history to give himself some sort of victory.

Tiger certainly wasn't bashful about his fondness for winning, even in front of strangers. During the taping of a segment for a TV news magazine in Los Angeles, Tiger played a nine-hole match against a reporter. At the end of the match, which Tiger won by six shots (33 to 39), the reporter asked Tiger why he liked competing so much. Tiger answered, 'Because I just love competition.' Then the reporter noted that Tiger usually wins everything he does on the golf course. Tiger matter-of-factly replied, 'Yeah, just like today. I beat you.'

The full swing is a continuation of the less-than-full swing's turn-and-slap motion. You use the full swing to hit the ball the maximum distance you can with a particular club, and to do that you need a greater range of motion than you achieve with a less-than-full swing motion. Your maximum range in the less-than-full swing was back to ten o'clock and through to two o'clock. In the full swing, your minimum range should be back to eleven o'clock and through to eleven o'clock. To find your optimum swing length in the full swing, keep swinging bigger and bigger until you begin to fall off balance. The maximum length of your swing should be the points, on the backswing and the follow-through, at which you begin to fall off balance.

Before beginning to work with the five steps in this chapter, it's important to erase from memory any preconceived notion of what a big swing should be. For example, some golfers believe the club should be parallel at the top of the backswing. In fact, it *should* be parallel – but only if that's as far as you can swing while staying in balance. Your swing goes back as far as it will go, and through as far as it will go. The length of your swing should be solely dependent on your individual elasticity and suppleness.

There are no perfect places for a backswing and a follow-through to stop, but there is perfect balance. At the end of the backswing, your weight should be over the top of your right foot – if you are right-handed – and that foot should be resting flat on the ground. At the end of the follow-through, your weight should be over the top of your left foot, with the left foot flat on the ground.

Many professionals roll out their left foot a little during the follow-through, so the inside edge of the foot is slightly off the ground at the end of the follow-through. That's OK, but at the beginning of your full-swing development I suggest that you keep your left foot grounded to help you stay in balance.

It's tempting to envy graceful and powerful swings. But don't be a copycat, because copycats don't become good golfers, or good anythings, for that matter. There's a perfect size golf swing just for you, and you will learn that swing – and play good golf with it – by gradually progressing through my five-step programme.

Some golfers stay in perfect balance throughout an enormous swing, going back past twelve o'clock and through past twelve o'clock. Phil Mickelson is a good example. He swings back to at least one o'clock and through to at least one o'clock, but he is usually well balanced. On the other hand, Paul Azinger rarely, if ever, reaches twelve o'clock in either direction, yet he has won twelve PGA Tour events, including the '93 PGA Championship, and has been on four Ryder Cup teams.

The engine of the full swing is a sequence of motions that involve the twisting and turning of your body. As the body turns, it moves the arms, which move the hands. The hands are holding the club, and as a result of the body turn, the club runs into the ball and propels it up and forwards. Remember: the club goes where the body takes it.

During the backswing, you turn your torso to the right, or away from the target – if you are right-handed – so your weight shifts to be over your right foot. At this point, your back faces the target and your chest faces away from the target. You then begin to turn back towards the target, ending with your chest facing the target. During this back-and-forth twisting motion, the arms, hands and club should all be submissive, responding to where the torso makes them go.

ROCK 'N' ROPE

I use a training aid that replicates a rope with a rock attached to the end of it to demonstrate how a clubhead is supposed to swing around the torso, or body. Using the rock-and-rope device gives students the feel of the clubhead's movement during the swing. In fact, the clubhead is the fastest moving part of the swing, and it's also the part of the club farthest away from the body during the swing. Centrifugal force, not strength, keeps the clubhead moving around the body during the swing, and it's easy to really feel the force with the rock-and-rope image.

Think of your arms, hands and the shaft as if they are connected to each other, together forming a piece of rope, which is attached to your torso. The clubhead is the rock. The turning of your torso generates the energy that powers the rope, and, in turn, the rope powers the rock.

It wasn't until I had been teaching golf for many years that I learned the value of the rock-and-rope device to simulate the swing and teach students how to feel the swing. But once I understood this visual image and used the device, I began hitting the ball straighter and longer because I was no longer trying to manipulate the clubhead. Rather, I knew that if I properly addressed the ball and then made a proper body turn, I had no other option but to hit the ball correctly.

HOW TO SEE GOOD BALANCE

It's easiest to understand balance by feeling it, but you can also see the difference between bad and good balance. At the end of the follow-through, a well-balanced golfer has her or his torso vertically stacked up in a straight line.

Here are some other visual images that indicate good balance at the end of a swing.

- The left foot is flat on the ground.
- The left ankle is aligned vertically with the left foot, and is not twisted or bent.
- The left knee is slightly flexed and directly over the left ankle.
- The hips are directly above the knees and are not sticking out. The hips should be level, meaning one hip should not be noticeably higher than the other.
- Each shoulder is directly above its respective hip.
- The head is erect, facing directly at the target and centred in between the shoulders – not lagging over towards one shoulder.

This image of your body at the end of the follow-through is the resting position you should strive to have at the conclusion of all motions, including less-than-full swings and full swings. Unless you have to swing around tree limbs, or are in another unusual predicament, you should never make a swing motion that compromises perfect balance at any point in the swing.

Finally, I want to restate one of my most important suggestions: don't measure yourself on bad shots. They are not you. Any swing that isn't in perfect balance is not worth evaluating. Trust me: you won't learn to play great golf by evaluating bad swings.

All swing motions should employ basically the same technique, whether you're hitting a chip, a mid-iron or a driver. The only thing that changes from shot to shot is the size of the swing and the width of your stance. So in this chapter, we're not going to add much technique to the less-than-full swing. Instead, we're mostly going to add size to the swing, and groove this expanded motion.

Here are the five steps for the full swing.

> STEP 1: Alignment
> STEP 2: A swing for all clubs
> STEP 3: A mixed bag
> STEP 4: Success training
> STEP 5: Play away and have fun

STEP 1: ALIGNMENT

Objective: To learn the basics of full-swing alignment.

Lesson: The full swing involves hitting the ball long distances with big power, and specific alignment is essential. With the full swing the ball usually travels over 100 yards, and thus has much more energy than it does in shorter shots. The extra energy makes the ball travel fast, therefore causing it to spin fast, and any sidespin the ball has will now cause the ball to curve. In short shots, the ball isn't travelling fast enough to spin enough to curve much. That's why it's very difficult to hit a 50-yard shot with lots of curve.

This step provides basic alignment principles that you will use for your entire career. You might vary the length or speed of your swing at different points in your career, but alignment should remain constant. Alignment is golf's version of a road map, and as you know, road maps rarely change.

TIMELESS BEAUTY

I have a collection of videos that I made of Tiger golfing when he was a child. It's fun to compare the old videos with current videos, and to see how his swing is virtually the same today as it was when he was four years old. His follow-through balance position is exactly the same as it was when he was little. Then and now, he's at full height, perfectly balanced on his left foot, facing the target, and his wrists and elbows are bent and close

to his chest. He also has a sense of softness in his finish position,
even though the swing produced a powerful shot.

THE ALIGNMENT GRID

All motion in the golf swing reacts to your alignment. However, there are many different types of alignment that are acceptable, so long as the golfer swings in sync with his alignment and thus solidly hits the ball at the target. Proper alignment doesn't necessarily mean lining up directly with your target. Lee Trevino lined up well left of his target, and Miller Barber lined up well to the right; but both players had swings that were perfectly in sync with their alignment, and their swings produced ball flights that curved the ball towards the target.

I'm going to give you my basic alignment preference. This alignment position matches the swing motion that I'm teaching you. Once you've learned this basic swing motion and alignment, it would be perfectly OK to adjust them to your personal feel.

There is an ideal alignment in golf that, with a robot, will produce the most powerful swing possible. However, golfers aren't robots, and they don't always swing perfectly. That's why a golfer could have perfect alignment but rarely hit the ball at the target because he doesn't make a swing motion that matches his alignment. It would be like improperly placing an arrow on a bow. No matter how strong the bow is, it won't shoot an arrow very far unless the arrow is perfectly positioned.

On the other hand, a golfer might line up crooked – like Barber and Trevino – but make a swing motion that matches his alignment. That swing will, most often, include some compensating moves to make the ball fly at the target. So although the swing might not be as powerful and efficient as it could be, with perfect alignment, the golfer swings well enough to be a good player.

Go to the practice range and set up an alignment grid on the ground. To make the grid, you can use golf clubs, surveyor tape, plumb line chalk, yardsticks – anything that's flat, at least a few feet long and straight. I prefer white surveyor tape, which you can purchase at most hardware stores.

The grid will include two lines. One line points directly at the target. I call that the target line, while other teachers call it the toe line. The other line is perpendicular to the target line, and is used to determine ball location relative to your body in the address position. Each line should be approximately 3 feet long. Together, the lines form a plus sign (+).

Set up a grid in the area in which you will stand to hit shots. If you use surveyor tape, peg the tape into the turf with tees. If you are right-handed, your left foot should be on the target side of the ball-position line, and your right foot should be on the other side of the line. There should be a one-clubhead gap between your left foot and the ball-position line. This distance remains constant for almost every shot, regardless of the club; however, the distance between your right foot and the ball-position line varies, depending on the type of shot. Generally, the bigger the shot, the more the right foot moves away from the ball-position line. Find stance sizes for different shots that feel comfortable, but be sure that you stay in perfect balance throughout the swing.

Never adjust the target-side foot. In all swings, you keep the left foot fixed, about one clubhead to the left of the target side of the ball, because the body pivots over the left foot. If the left foot doesn't remain constant from shot to shot relative to the ball's location, you'll constantly have to readjust your pivot point to hit the ball, and doing that is almost impossible.

BALL POSITION

The ball should be teed up a few inches away from the end of the ball-position line. The ball should be a little closer to your body for short wedge shots, and a little farther away for drives. That's because your wedge is the shortest club and the driver is the longest club. You adjust the distance the ball sits from your body at address, depending on the size of the shot. Using this rule, the longer the shot, the farther away the ball is from your body.

FEET POSITION

At address, each foot should be the same distance from the target line. If you are right-handed, your right foot should be almost perpendicular to the target line. Your left foot should be 'open', turned a little towards the target. Adjust your feet so that you are comfortable and balanced.

IT'S TIME TO HIT SOME SHOTS

Take a 7-iron and a bucket of practice balls and go to the practice tee. Tee up two practice balls next to each other. Each ball should be slightly above the turf, replicating a perfect lie. Set up a grid, and get into the address position over the grid. Make as full a swing as possible, but use a small amount of power to hit each ball. It should feel like you're swinging in slow motion. The goal is to achieve a full range of motion and stay balanced throughout the swing. How far the ball goes is irrelevant.

Hit a few shots with this full but purposely slow swing. Remember, the arms, hands and shaft are the rope and the clubhead is the rock on the end of the rope. Rotate your torso all the way back and all the way through and stay in balance, and the club will go where the body directs it.

Swing and hit each ball, finishing in perfect balance and facing the target. Hit balls in sets of two so you'll be forced to step away and reorient yourself after every couple of shots. In the finish position, your knees should be almost touching or touching. Either position is OK. At the conclusion of each shot, check your balance.

● Is your torso stacked up in a straight line and over the left foot?
● Did you turn and slap the ball?

At this stage of your golf development, you should tee up every shot on the range so you don't have to worry about the lie. I want all of your concentration to go into your balance and the swing motion. You can learn to hit from different lies after you perfect the swing motion.

Skill
requirement: Using a 7-iron (or the closest iron you have to a 7-iron), hit a total of at least 250 balls over at least three different sessions. Use the grid with a full swing but less-than-full power. Hit shots in sets of two, teeing up two balls and then stepping away from the grid after each set. Don't change clubs.

STEP 2: A SWING FOR ALL CLUBS

Objective: To hit full-swing shots with every club in your bag.

Lesson: How do you control the flight of your golf ball? *Not by manipulating the clubhead during the swing*. You control the ball by making a correct swing motion.

The correct motion for the full swing is the same as the motion for the less-than-full swing, except you go back farther and follow through farther. The increased range of motion gives the swing more power. At Step 2 in the Less-than-Full Swing chapter, you learned to turn your torso back and away from the target, allowing your wrists to bend as you went back to the nine o'clock position. Make the same initial motion here, but go back to eleven or twelve o'clock, so the club is almost parallel to the ground and pointing at the target at the end of the backswing. As the shoulders horizontally turn away from the target, your arms and hands simultaneously glide away from the target and up towards the sky.

You don't have to keep your head in a fixed position throughout the swing. The saying, 'Keep your head down,' is one of the great fallacies of the game. You don't have to keep your head down to hit good golf shots. Trying to keep your head down is actually bad, because it forces golfers to restrict their natural swing motions. Don't worry where your head goes during the swing; it'll go where the body takes it, and wherever that may be is just fine.

HOW TO BE A STRAIGHT ARROW

Rotating or turning the torso towards the target prevents the ball from going right. The fact that you're turning and swinging the club around your body won't allow the clubface to be open – facing to the right if you are right-handed – at impact, and that assures no ball will veer to the right.

To keep the ball from going too far left, or hooking, you need to have a natural release and maintain perfect balance over your left foot. This left-foot balance is also called a 'firm left side'. So you should turn and slap from the side – making a motion like a baseball pitcher throwing sidearmed – and this keeps the clubface from closing at impact and thus hooking the ball to the left.

At address, your toe line should point directly at the target, but your clubface should face a tiny bit to the right of the target, if you are right-handed. The clubface points a shade to the right of where the toe line faces because a good shot with the full swing is going to curve slightly from right to left. On a perfect shot, the ball will curve, or draw, about three feet to the left.

The ball curves because the toe of the clubhead, at the moment of impact, is turning from right to left. That puts a little sideways spin on the ball, causing it to twist from right to left as it flies. You shouldn't try to turn the clubhead. The clubhead turns naturally as a result of making a proper release motion.

DISTANCE CONTROL

In golf, you have to hit the ball different distances, and you usually don't do that by using one club with a bunch of different swings. Instead, you use one swing with a lot of different clubs. Each club has a unique design – determined by its loft, lie, weight and shaft length – and the unique design makes the ball go certain distances, with a good swing.

Of course, you can play golf with just one club, say a 5-iron, by changing your swing to make the 5-iron hit different distances. In fact, there's a one-club national championship, and the winner usually shoots below 80. But golfers tend to lose their tempo and balance when creating shots that a club isn't designed to hit. For example, I can naturally hit my 5-iron 170 yards, and I can, if necessary, hit the 5-iron as far as 180 yards. But when I make the 180-yard swing with the 5-iron, I have trouble staying balanced and my success rate drops.

GOING THROUGH THE BAG

Bring your bag and grid materials to the practice range and set up a grid. You're going to tee up two balls, hit them, and then tee up two more. Hit four shots with each club, starting with the sand wedge and progressing through the irons and then to the woods. Don't worry about the shot quality. You might hit three good 7-irons out of four and only one good 3-wood out of four.

This exercise is designed to teach you to get used to hitting each of your different clubs, as you must do in a real round. After you finish the driver, go back to the sand wedge and go through your bag again. At each practice session, you should go through the entire bag twice. I suggest doing this drill until you feel perfectly comfortable hitting every club. You don't have to hit them all well, but you can't be afraid of a single club. A good swing motion will produce a good shot with every club in the bag.

I CAN'T HIT MY LONG IRONS!

Here's a complaint that I commonly hear from students: 'I hit my short irons great, but I'm terrible with the long irons.' My reply is always the same: 'How often do you practise your long irons?' Usually the answer is, 'Never.' How can you become proficient with every club if you don't practise with every club? Practise.

Skill requirement: In a single session at the range, hit at least two good shots with every club in your bag using a full swing. You should hit one shot at a time and change clubs after every shot. Start with the wedges, move on to the 9-iron and then progress through the irons. Then hit your woods, beginning with your highest-numbered wood. After hitting two good shots with a club, put the club to the side. Do this drill on two different days and you have finished Step 2.

STEP 3: A MIXED BAG

Objectives: (1) To hit shots with each club in no particular order; and (2) to begin hitting shots without teeing them up.

Lesson: In Step 1 you only used a 7-iron, and in Step 2 you hit full swings with all your clubs, going through your bag in order. Now you're going to take the previous concepts a level further by alternating back and forth between clubs in no particular order. For example, you'll switch from a wedge to a 3-wood to a 5-iron to a driver as you practise on the range.

Mixing up the rotation of clubs during practice might seem trivial, but it's an essential skill that many beginners gloss over. In real golf, you rarely hit the same club two times in succession – except on the putting green – and you want practice to mimic reality as much as possible.

Go to the range with two buckets of practice balls and your bag. You can pretend you're at a course that you've played a few times so you can visualise shots that you want to practise. You're going to play imaginary holes, hitting every shot on each hole except for putts and bunker shots. You don't have to start at the first hole. Simply begin at the hole that you best remember on the course.

Hit your tee shot. While holding your finish, check your balance and watch your ball. Gauge where the ball would have ended up on the hole you've imagined. Hit your next shot and continue hitting until you reach the green. Give yourself two putts and go to the next hole. Play at least nine imaginary holes.

CLEANING OUT MY BAG

When I was an aspiring tour pro, I took lessons from John Revolta, who had been a top Tour player before he became a teacher. At the conclusion of my first lesson, every club I owned was leaning against my bag. I hadn't realised it, but I'd hit every single club in my bag during that lesson, and I did the same during almost every other lesson I took from John.

I do the same with my students, making them use each club during a lesson, because too many golfers learn to play the game by hitting just a couple clubs. They become proficient with these clubs, but they don't get used to their other clubs, and when it's time to play golf, they are often afraid of hitting many of their clubs.

SPLITTING TIME BETWEEN THE RANGE AND THE COURSE

As you progress through each step in this chapter, you are building a total golf game, developing your swing and the intangible skills necessary to play good golf. Of course, you should play golf, but you have to balance your time on the course with time on the practice tee. What's more, hitting on the practice tee provides an atmosphere that is less pressurised than the course, because there's no temptation to keep score and judge your progress.

You should still be playing imaginary holes on the range. Make each swing you take a full one, going as far back and as far through as possible, and try to stay in perfect balance from beginning to end. As I've said, no two golfers own the same swing, and there is no perfect swing. A key goal as you learn to play is to become intimately familiar with your swing, what it feels like, why it works and what you need to do to fix it when it doesn't work. An excellent way to learn about your swing is to vary your swing from shot to shot while practising.

In your mind, determine what you think is the ideal size of your swing in terms of its length. Then hit some shots in which you purposely swing longer than normal and other shots in which you purposely swing shorter than normal. Continue varying the size of your swing and the position of your hands on the grip with each club in your bag, including your driver. Doing this not only will teach you about your swing, but you will also learn what is too long and too short a swing for you.

In this step, I suggest that you begin to hit some shots off the turf. Also remove the ball-position tape from the grid. By now, ball position probably will have started to become instinctive. Remember, the ball should be one clubhead inside your left foot with all clubs. If you lose the feel for proper positioning of the ball, use the tape for a while longer. (I suggest you keep tape in your bag and practise with it throughout your career. Everybody can use an alignment reminder once in a while.)

Hitting off the turf is really no different from hitting off the tee. Off the turf, you use the same swing motion as you did with a tee, and the club will hit the ball just fine off the ground. Don't change anything in the swing or set-up. Whatever you were doing off the tee, do the same things without the tee. A helpful hint is to pretend that the ball is on a tee.

Moving the ball off the tee to the turf might cause you to develop some anxiety about not being able to get the ball airborne. I can appreciate that concern because it's a common fear, and I've had it myself. But the truth is, golf clubs have more than enough loft and other design features to propel the ball into the air with a normal swing. Golfers have a myriad of plasters to overcome the anxiety of hitting off the turf. They include watching the top of the ball or the back of the ball; keeping your head down until you see the turf under the ball; and keeping your head still throughout the swing. Such plasters may or may not work. However, employing the same exact swing you used when hitting off a tee always works.

HOW TO KEEP THINGS INTERESTING

Tiger was already proficient at hitting with every club when he was five years old so, in effect, he was already an expert. He needed to refine his game, not find a new one. We would begin our lessons on the range, but after watching Tiger hit about thirty shots it was obvious that we didn't need to work on his technique. So we'd go off to the course, which is where we both really wanted to be anyway.

The goal of golf is to play the game and have fun. While playing, friends and I will sometimes discuss strategy for specific shots. We'll think of different ways to hit a shot and then try each method. It's a good idea to vary your routine on the course. On a hole where you would normally hit a driver off the tee, try hitting a 3-iron. See how the new strategy affects your score. You might make a good score and be surprised.

The only two things that every golfer must do are play by the rules and keep up with the group ahead. Other than that, every golfer needs to individualise the game, and discover, through trial and error, the activities and routines that help him play well and have fun.

POSTURE
Golf is definitely a motion sport, and you need to have proper posture to make an athletic motion for the swing. This athletic motion, though, is usually overdone. Golfers make it more complex than it needs to be. I tell golfers they should treat the swing like a parent lifting a baby in and out of a car seat. That lifting is an athletic motion, yet the parent doesn't get in a contrived position prior to picking up the baby. The parent just instinctively prepares his or her body to lift the weight of the child. Likewise, you should instinctively prepare your body to make a golf swing motion, and not be concerned with the 1,001 muscle movements you think are necessary to hit the ball. Of course, you have to learn a few basic principles about the swing, but once you've learned the basics, the general motion needs to become mostly instinctive if you want to play well.

Regarding posture in golf, the first key point is that you need to slightly tilt forwards at the hips. Also, your knees should have just a little bit of flex; your weight should be evenly distributed between both feet; your head should sit comfortably on top of your shoulders; and your arms hang down from your shoulders. You should also be looking down at the ball. The biggest error I see with posture is a deep knee bend. You don't need to reach down or squat to be in a proper address position. If anything, you would tilt over a little more at the hips to get low enough to put the clubhead on the ground behind the ball.

Use the same address position with all clubs.

*Skill
requirement*:   Pick any club and hit two balls at a predetermined
target. Do this with every club in your bag. Use
full swings and hit off the turf. Do this for two
separate sessions, going through your bag twice in
each session. You should hit at least 50 per cent
of your shots well. If you do this successfully,
you've completed Step 3.

STEP 4: SUCCESS TRAINING

Objective: To play nine-hole rounds hitting at least one good
shot from every position your ball lands in.

Lesson: By now you should have established your basic
full swing motion. You can swing every club in the
bag; you understand what makes the ball go right
and left; and you can feel the difference between
a good swing and a bad swing.

Now you're ready to move your practice sessions to the golf
course. Play during the least busy times, because you will be
hitting multiple shots from the same location, and you don't
want to worry about pace of play.

In Step 3, you began making the transition from practice to
playing by hitting shots with different clubs in no particular
order, and by playing imaginary holes on the practice tee.
You're going to continue the transition with my Success
Training drill. I also call this the Personal Scramble.

You should play nine holes. You can play alone or with
somebody, as long as your partner is patient. Your goal is to hit
a good shot from every position before moving to the next
position on a hole. If you hit a bad shot, put down another ball
and hit again. (Don't forget to pick up your bad shots.) Keep
hitting until you hit a good shot. Then walk to where the good
shot stopped and play your next shot from that position. Feel
free to tee up your ball throughout the round if it makes you
more comfortable. You are only making the transition from the
range to the course; you're not learning to cheat.

The most important rule of this drill is to finish every hole (unless you have to pick up to maintain a proper pace of play). The drill will help you to develop a sense for the kind of shots you're capable of hitting if things go well. In success training, a 25-handicapper can easily break 80, and single-digit handicappers should be able to shoot in the mid to low 60s.

Here's how to play a Personal Scramble. If you're on a par 3 and you top your first shot into the water and your second shot hits the green, the second shot is the one you count. Once on the green, you hit your first putt 25 feet past the hole. Drop another ball and hit the first putt again. If the second putt stops 6 feet from the hole, that's the one you play. You putt the 6-footer into the hole, and you've made a three. Put three down on the scorecard.

There's no standardised set of rules for the Personal Scramble. Use your judgment as to how many attempts you need from each position. Generally, I don't keep hitting until I've hit a perfect shot. Rather, I hit until I hit a good shot. On the greens, I'll give myself two or three attempts at each putt.

HOW TO IMPROVE? MORE PRACTICE, NOT NEW TECHNIQUES

Doing the Personal Scramble drill should teach you that playing well isn't primarily dependent on improving your swing. By now, you're probably capable of hitting excellent shots, which means you have a good swing. The problem is that you don't always use that good swing.

You need to develop the awareness that you're capable of hitting excellent shots, and the Personal Scramble is the best way to do that. How can the same golfer who topped a ball then hit the next shot on to the green? In school, a maths teacher might require you to practise adding single-digit numbers for a few weeks until you've mastered the technique. The same diligence is necessary to become a good golfer. Repetition teaches you how to make good swings.

Skill   Play two nine-hole rounds using the Personal
requirement: Scramble, hitting no more than three shots from
                 each location. The only other requirement is that
                 you hit at least one good shot with every club in
                 your bag during each round.

STEP 5: PLAY AWAY AND HAVE FUN

Objective: To play an 18-hole round, hitting into the hole on
                 every green.

Lesson: Welcome to playing golf. You've developed all the
                 skills that are necessary to play golf, and you're
                 ready to play a traditional nine-hole round, play-
                 ing each shot as it lies, putting out and abiding by
                 the Rules of Golf.

You should play with a parent or a friend to maximise your
comfort level. As you did in Step 4, play when the course isn't
too busy, on a weekday or a weekend in the late afternoon. For
your first round, hit every shot off the turf, except on the tee
boxes.

You can keep score, but don't be concerned about it. The goal
of playing this round is to apply all the skills that you've
learned. It's not to shoot a specific score. If you have a big
problem on any hole, pick up and go to the next hole. At this
point in your career, it is perfectly acceptable to not finish every
hole. There is nothing to ever be embarrassed about on the golf
course, unless you cheat or don't use good etiquette.

OVERWHELMED BY FEAR

*I know somebody whose fear of being embarrassed on the
course overwhelms his desire to play, and has kept him away
from the course for years. The golfer is a man in his early
forties. He's an excellent all-around athlete, a black belt in
karate who has played basketball in a competitive league. He's
not a very good golfer, but he took up the game because he had
friends who took him out to play.*

After playing for a while, the man developed a huge fear about what other people thought of him on the first tee. He felt that he had to hit a good shot to prove himself. Eventually, his jitters became so overwhelming that he decided he'd rather stay home than face the first tee. The man has told me that he would like to start playing again, but he's so worried about the possibilities of hitting a bad shot on the first tee in front of other people that he has chosen not even to visit the course.

Continue playing nine-hole rounds, picking the ball up when things don't go well, until you can complete a round without ever having to pick up your ball. Then you're ready to try 18 holes. It's always OK to pick up your ball and move to the next tee, but you want to work towards never having to pick up. When you can play 18 holes without a single pick-up, you're a bona fide golfer. You're ready to play anywhere, from Augusta National to Golden Pebble, a course near Beijing, China, that has a few waterfront holes as dramatic and beautiful as the oceanside holes at Pebble Beach in California.

At this point, you're as much a golfer as the best players in the world. The only difference is that your scores are higher. But the difference in score should not affect your enjoyment of the game.

TOURNAMENT GOLF: YOUR DECISION

You know how to play golf. If you've progressed all the way through my programme, and fulfilled each skill requirement and taken every quiz, you should be proud of yourself. In golf, as in life, it's important to pat yourself on the back once in a while.

You now might be thinking about pursuing tournament golf. It's going to take a lot of time and effort to get your game in the shape necessary to compete whether you play on a city, state or national level. But if you've enjoyed the learning process so far, then now's a good time to get serious. I've always enjoyed the competitive aspects of golf, and I often compete in club professional tournaments. If you're considering starting on the long road that it takes to become a tournament player, I assure you that the rewards will far outweigh the sacrifices.

You're going to enjoy the game whether you decide to pursue tournament golf or to casually play with your friends. Both options are good. Whichever choice you make, score alone should never affect your enjoyment. That may sound impossible, but it's not. I often tell golfers, 'If you're not having fun today, what makes you think that you'll have fun tomorrow?'

They often say that they'll be happier when they score better. Wrong! Better scores usually have the opposite effect. Golfers are greedy, and as they begin to shoot lower, their expectations rise. So the game becomes a never-ending quest for enjoyment through lower scores. Don't get caught in this trap, or you'll feel like a mouse on a treadmill.

I'm not preaching, but I am being honest. No golfer will ever be happy as long as her or his happiness is tied to a score. I know, because my enjoyment was attached to my score for too long. Years ago, I was happy if I hit a good shot or had a low score. If I hit a bad shot or shot a high score, I was miserable.

Eventually, I began to ask myself, 'Why am I spending so much time pursuing something that makes me miserable a lot of the time?' It took a while, but I eventually learned my lesson. Real fun in golf comes from enjoying the process of trying to shoot a lower score, the environment, playing partners and the other wonderful elements of the game.

DAD'S BAD ATTITUDE

I was 14 years old when my father, Rudy, introduced me to golf. We occasionally played golf together, and Dad had more bad rounds than good ones. After a bad round, he'd be so upset that he would go straight home, get undressed, crawl into the bathtub and fill it with steaming water up to his neck. Fuming, Dad would lie in the tub for hours. He often missed dinner. Nobody could talk to Dad after a bad round.

It was obvious that Dad wasn't having fun on the course.

Today, I realise that a terrible attitude kept my father from being as good a player as he could have become. He turned 77 in 2000, but he is a much better golfer now than he was at 40 years old. Today his handicap is 12, and 40 years ago it was 19. Now Dad has fun on his good days and his bad days. I often wonder how good Dad would've become if he had appreciated and enjoyed golf in the old days like he does now.

Don't let this happen to you. There are a lot of wonderful things in golf. Don't miss out on experiencing the joys the game has to offer because of a bad attitude. If you're going to rant and rave over every bad shot, you won't find the pleasure that golf has to offer.

Working with Tiger helped me learn this lesson. Even when Tiger was four years old, I noticed that he enjoyed himself regardless of his score. No matter how many times he swung the club, he always (well, almost always) smiled.

Remember the experience I described in Chapter 1, in which Tiger, just ten years old, scored a 10 on a hole but still had a great day? I vividly recall stopping for burgers at McDonald's on the way home, and Tiger was happy because he felt that he'd had a great day playing golf. It wasn't until a few days after the round that I realised that when we were at McDonald's discussing the round, we talked mostly about the good shots and we laughed about the bad ones.

The fact that Tiger plays golf for fun is one of the big reasons why he dominates his competition. During a tournament, he doesn't think about how tough the course is, how his competitors are playing or about whether he's going to win. He's trying to do the best he can on every swing, and to him, that's a ton of fun. Even with his great shot-making ability, I think if Tiger didn't have so much fun on the golf course, he would be much less motivated to improve, and he might not be so successful.

Skill requirement: Play one 18-hole round, hitting into the cup on every hole. Smile as you walk off *every* green. You can keep score if you like, but it is not necessary.

8. GENERAL KNOWLEDGE

EVERYTHING YOU NEED TO KNOW ABOUT GOLF – EXCEPT TECHNIQUE

This chapter has nothing to do with how to hit the golf ball. It does, however, have everything to do with the game of golf and its unique language. After reading this chapter, you'll be able to talk the talk of golf, whether you're at the pro shop, driving range, caddie shack or 19th hole. You'll know the difference between a parkland-style golf course and a links. You'll know how to make a tee time and where to buy equipment. And you'll know several 'insider tips', including how to play golf at private country clubs for free.

I had a female student in her mid-thirties who'd been playing for a few years and was a member at a private country club. A left-hander, she was hitting way left, and I asked her, 'Do you know why you're fading the ball?'

She gave me a puzzled look, and I asked if she knew what a fade is. 'Umm, well, what's that?' she said.

I was stunned. Here was somebody who had played golf for years but didn't know one of the game's most basic terms. That experience was a revelation. It showed me that even seasoned golfers don't know the game's ABCs, and that's a shame. It's impossible to appreciate the game fully or to communicate with a teacher or your playing partners if you don't speak the same language.

Consider this hypothetical situation. A low-handicap golfer is about to begin tenth grade at a new school. Her family gets delayed while moving, so the girl misses orientation and the first week of classes. A month into the semester, the girl's best friend tells her how much she likes her sculpture class and that she'd played great in try-outs for the girls' golf team. The new student is dumbfounded. *The school has a sculpture class and a girls' golf team?* The new student loves golf and sculpture, but she didn't know about the class or the team, so she missed out on her favourite activities.

The same thing often happens to golfers who aren't informed about the game, no matter how well they might play. Perhaps a golfer would miss a fun two-person team tournament because he didn't know to look on the tournament bulletin board at his club. Or the golfer will break his club while hitting off an asphalt cart path because he didn't know that the rules would've permitted a free drop.

Knowing the ins and outs of golf will definitely make you feel at home around the course. That will probably put you in a good mood, and good moods usually translate into low scores.

Unlike the Putting, Less-than-Full Swing and Full Swing chapters, General Knowledge has no Skill requirement section. Instead, there are brief multiple-choice quizzes at the end of each step. The answer to each question is somewhere in this book, though not necessarily in this chapter. Have fun!

STEP 1: GOLF COURSE STAFF

GENERAL MANAGER

The general manager is in charge of a golf course and its business. Most golf courses are run like a business whose goal is to make a profit. Some courses are not-for-profit operations; they include private clubs owned by the members and courses owned by individuals. Regardless of the type of operation, the general manager assures that the course's staff and finances are expertly managed. Sometimes the general manager's duties are handled by the head golf professional. If you have any problem at a golf course, you first should try to speak with the general manager. If you can't get the general manager, go to the golf professional.

GOLF PROFESSIONAL

A golf professional is a man or a woman who gets paid for either playing in tournaments, giving lessons or managing a golf course. A tour professional plays in tournaments for a living and aspires to play on one of the many professional tours around the world. The major tours in the United States are the PGA

Tour (men), the Ladies Professional Golf Association (LPGA) and Senior Tour (men 50 and over). There are also significant tours based in Australia (men), Europe (men and women), Japan (men and women), South Africa (men), and there is an Asian tour for men. Club pros teach at and manage golf courses. Club pros are certified by the LPGA Teaching Division or the Professional Golfer's Association of America (PGA).

A club pro occasionally competes in tournaments, but spends most of her or his time organising club tournaments, giving lessons, running the pro shop and overseeing the golf carts and driving range. There are different levels of golf professionals. The boss is usually the director of golf. Her or his staff could include head pros, assistant pros, teaching pros and shop managers. LPGA- and PGA-certified members are required to go through lengthy training administered by their respective associations. Women can be an LPGA or PGA member, while men can only be in the PGA.

The PGA and the PGA Tour are independent organisations. The PGA oversees club professionals, while the PGA Tour owns and operates the PGA Tour, the Senior Tour and a developmental tour, which until 2001 was called the Buy.com Tour.

SUPERINTENDENT
The superintendent is responsible for the maintenance of the entire course grounds. He or she has to keep the grass green, the ponds and the car park clean and the greens smooth. Being a 'sup,' as superintendents are often called, is much more difficult and complex than most people realise. It's not easy to keep a 200-acre plot of rolling terrain, forest, water and other natural habitats looking beautiful 365 days a year. Top superintendents in the United States earn over $100,000 a year.

STARTER
The starter registers golfers for their tee times after they arrive at the course and calls them to the first tee a few minutes before they are to tee off. You should always check in with the starter prior to teeing off. If you don't check in at least 15 minutes before your tee time, you may lose it.

CADDIE

A caddie carries bags around the course for golfers. In addition to carrying the bag and hand-delivering clubs to his or her players, the caddie rakes bunkers and spots the balls. Caddies can be men or women (all caddies in Japan are women). They can be old (some are in their nineties) or young (around ten). They can be big people, like Herman Mitchell, who often weighed over 300 pounds and was Lee Trevino's former caddie, or small people, like Mitch Knox, who is skinny, 5ft 8in and has worked for David Duval for several years.

Caddies must be strong enough to carry the bags or push a bag on a cart, and they must understand the game and its rules. You don't have to be a good golfer to be a good caddie.

Some people caddie for a living, but caddying is also a great summer job. Some people caddie for fun, working for friends. When Tiger was ten years old, he caddied for me in the Long Beach Open, and in 2000 he caddied for his friend and former Stanford teammate, Jerry Chang, in the qualifying rounds at a USGA tournament.

One of the best perks of caddying is free golf. Most country clubs allow their caddies to play at no charge one day a week, usually Mondays, when the course is closed.

Caddies used to be prevalent at all courses in the United States. But motorised golf carts have become so popular that it's rare to find caddies anywhere in the United States. However, caddies are still widely used in Great Britain and Ireland.

MARSHAL

The marshal is the 'eye' of the pro shop out on the course. The marshal is in charge of maintaining safety, pace of play and proper etiquette. Years ago, a marshal at one of my courses saved somebody's life. After finding a golfer who'd had a heart attack, the marshal radioed the pro shop. The shop assistant called 911, and while waiting for the ambulance, the assistant went out to the course and administered CPR. The golfer survived and not too long afterwards was back at the course.

STEP 1: QUIZ

1. On what day are most private golf courses closed for maintenance?
   a. Monday
   b. Wednesday
   c. Friday

2. Jack Nicklaus holds the men's record for the most major championship victories. How many did he win?
   a. 28
   b. 5
   c. 18

3. What does a golf course builder primarily do?
   a. Sell pro shop merchandise
   b. Construct the clubhouse
   c. Shape holes and move dirt while a course is being built

4. Who can be a caddie?
   a. Anybody
   b. Men over 20 years old
   c. Good golfers

5. Whom should you look for if you have an emergency on the golf course?
   a. The police
   b. The marshal
   c. Your mother

6. In 2000, Tiger Woods set the record for margin of victory at the US Open. By how many strokes did Tiger win?
   a. 7
   b. 11
   c. 15

7. What's the busiest time at a golf course?
   a. Sunday afternoon
   b. Wednesday morning
   c. Saturday morning

8. With whom do you check in to confirm your tee time after arriving at the course?
   a. Starter
   b. Snack bar attendant
   c. Assistant pro

9. Which PGA Tour player has putted with his eyes closed?
   a. Ben Crenshaw
   b. Mark Calcavecchia
   c. Ernie Els

10. Who is responsible for maintaining the condition of a golf course?
    a. Superintendent
    b. Golf pro
    c. Marshal

Answers: 1. a; 2. c; 3. c; 4. c; 5. b; 6. c; 7. c; 8. a; 9. b; 10. a

STEP 2: THE FACILITY

PRO SHOP

The pro shop is the shop at the golf course that sells golf merchandise and clothing. It's also where you usually sign up for your round. Some pro shops are very well stocked with equipment, while other shops have a minimal selection. But all shops have the basics: balls, gloves, hats and tees.

The head pro's office is often in the pro shop. At older courses, the pro shop is not connected to the main clubhouse. The reason the pro shop and the clubhouse aren't connected provides insight into why golf has such an aristocratic reputation.

When golf first came to the United States, in the nineteenth century, professionals were held in low esteem by club members. Indeed, pros were not even allowed to enter the clubhouse or to socialise with the members. The pro, in essence, was a servant for the members, somebody giving them tips and running tournaments. That's why clubs constructed separate buildings for the pros, and these buildings became known as 'pro shops'.

It wasn't until around 1920 that golf pros, led by the flamboyant Walter 'The Haig' Hagen, began to stand up for pros' rights and gain for them respect – and the right to enter the clubhouse.

THE 'HAIG'

Walter Hagen loved rattling golf's upper crust, especially during his trips to the British Open. Here's a colourful snapshot depicting Hagen's antics, excerpted from a 1989 Sports Illustrated *article by Ron Fimrite.*

At his very first British Open, in 1920, at Deal, England, he [Hagen] arrived with 12 colour-co-ordinated golf outfits. He set up headquarters at the Ritz in London and hired an Austro-Daimler limousine and a footman. Disdaining the makeshift accommodations provided for the players, Hagen repaired to his limo and had the footman ostentatiously serve him lunch, with appropriate wines, inside the great machine. At another Open, he grandly hired an airplane and had himself flown 40 miles away to a fashionable inn where, he noisily proclaimed, the strawberries were infinitely superior to those served in the clubhouse. These adventures in one-upmanship were duly reported back home in the U.S. press. Hagen's boldness, bolstered by his mastery of the British Open, eventually carried the day. An incorrigible social climber, he somehow succeeded in charming the British upper crust, most notably the glamorous young Prince of Wales himself.

In the '20s, the Prince had become something of a golf groupie, and Hagen was his personal favourite. On one golf outing the Prince invited Hagen and Sarazen in for lunch at the Royal St. George's clubhouse. They were ready to order when an embarrassed steward begged his Highness's attention.

The rules of the club, he whispered, prohibit golf professionals from invading the dining area, even those in the company of such a distinguished guest. The future king of

England glared indignantly at the steward and said, in a voice that could be heard clearly by everyone inside, 'You stop this nonsense or I'll take the Royal out of St. George's.' Hagen and Sarazen were royally entertained.

DRIVING RANGE

The range is where you practise by hitting golf balls that you rent for a fee from the course or the range. The balls are available either in the pro shop or on the range, from a machine or an attendant. Range balls are to be used only on the range. You're not supposed to take them home or play on the course with them.

I belong to San Luis Obispo Country Club. The club's 14th hole is a 180-yard par 3 with a lake in front of the green, and our club cleans the lake every year. In 2000, the lake cleaners retrieved over 6,000 balls, and 5 per cent of them were range balls. Not even country club members are immune to the temptation to steal range balls.

PRACTICE GREEN AND PRACTICE BUNKER

Customers at my two courses in Central California often ask if they must pay to use the putting green, the chipping green and the practice bunker. No, they don't, nor would they have to pay at almost any public course. Indeed, you can practise at most public courses for free, even if you don't play a round.

Not all courses have practice greens and bunkers, but always ask the pro shop if you don't see such facilities. Sometimes they're hidden in out-of-the-way areas.

RESTAURANT

Not every golf course has a five-star restaurant, but most courses have some food service. The most primitive courses sell sweets in the pro shop, but most facilities have at least a snack bar or set of vending machines. At the other end of the spectrum are courses with fancy restaurants and huge ballrooms that cater for weddings and large parties. Lots of courses also have snack stands on the course, or roving food carts, so you can get something to eat during your round without detouring into the clubhouse. Bring cash for the snack stands and food carts, because they rarely accept credit cards.

THE GOLF COURSE

PARTS OF THE COURSE

The golf course is composed of individual holes, ranging from one to 18. Generally, courses have nine or 18 holes. Each hole has a tee, a fairway and a green. The tee is the starting point for a hole. The fairway is the short grass between the tee and the green, and it's where you're supposed to hit your ball to from the tee on par 4s and par 5s. The green has the shortest grass on the course and is where the hole is located.

Golf holes can have rough (thick grass along the fairway), water, rock gardens, sand bunkers, waste areas, trees and other obstacles that you have to negotiate over and around to get your ball from the tee into the hole.

LITTLE TIGER STANDING TALL

When Tiger was six, he and I played a round at the Navy course in Cypress, California. We were on the seventh tee and Tiger's ball was dirty. Most kids don't care if their ball is sparkling white or covered in mud, but Tiger always wanted his ball to be perfectly clean.

I was sitting on a bench by the seventh tee, and Tiger walked behind my back towards the ball washer. It seemed like a long time passed, maybe a minute, and Tiger still didn't return. I turned around and my eyes almost popped out. There was Tiger, a tiny kid, straddling the ball washer, which was taller than he was. He had one arm around the washer, and his other arm was stretched up and over the top of the washer, pumping up and down to clean his ball. To reach the washing mechanism, Tiger was standing on the little steel protrusion sticking out from the bottom of the pole that doubled as a spike cleaner.

I have videotape of Tiger washing his ball that day. Every time I watch the video, I get sentimental because the memory is endearing. It shows the effort kids have to go through to live in an adult world, particularly on golf courses, where nothing seems built to fit them.

TYPES OF COURSES

There are three types of golf courses: executive, par 3 and regulation. Regulation layouts have a par between 70 and 72 and a combination of par 3, par 4 and par 5 holes. An executive course has a par of less than 70 and consists mostly of par 3s and par 4s. Very few executive courses have par 5s. A par 3 course contains only par 3s. Any of these three types of courses can have nine or 18 holes.

If your kids are under ten, a par 3 or executive course would be an ideal place to play, no matter how skilled they are. One reason Tiger's parents brought their son to me was that I worked at a par 3 course, Heartwell Park, in Long Beach. A big advantage of executive and par 3 courses is that you can play 18 holes in less than two hours, the time it often takes for nine holes at a regulation course.

COURSE DESIGN STYLES

Parkland: A course that has lots of trees and replicates a forested, parklike setting. Each hole is surrounded by trees. Augusta National Golf Club in Georgia, the home of the Masters tournament, is a parkland layout.

Links: In Great Britain, where golf began, a links is a course on sandy terrain with few or no trees, and the land is located directly next to the sea. The term *links* later became a nickname for a golf course, regardless of its location or design style. Eventually, golfers outside Great Britain began naming courses 'links'. Modern links throughout the world are often similar in style to native links in Britain, with one exception: they are often not situated at the seaside.

To me, a true links isn't defined by its proximity to water. Rather, a links is a course that you can play from tee to green with a putter. Alister MacKenzie, a famous Scottish architect, said, 'No hole can be considered perfect unless it can be played with a putter.'

Target: Target courses are generally found in desert or swampy regions. A target course, I believe, is the most challenging type of design because it offers all-or-nothing consequences on many shots.

On each hole, you usually hit from an irrigated area of grassy terrain over native landscape (i.e. marshland, water or some other hazard) to another irrigated grassy area. Target golf is difficult, because there are so many forced carries over unplayable areas.

The world's most famous target course is the TPC at Sawgrass in Ponte Vedra Beach, Florida. Designed by Pete Dye, Sawgrass hosts the Players Championship, a prestigious PGA Tour event, and is home to one of the world's most famous holes, the infamous par 3 seventeenth, with its island green.

STEP 2: QUIZ
1. What are dewsweepers?
   a. The people who cut the greens in the morning
   b. The first players on a course in the morning
   c. Machines that sweep moisture off a green

2. How many attempts can you take on each shot while playing a personal scramble?
   a. As many as it takes to hit a good shot
   b. Three
   c. One

3. What is a beach?
   a. Edge of a water hazard
   b. Sand bunker
   c. Room in the clubhouse in which you relax after playing golf

4. How many par 5 holes do executive courses have?
   a. 2
   b. 4
   c. 0

5. What is Lee Trevino's nickname?
   a. Merry Mex
   b. The Squire
   c. The Golden Bear

6. Where should you stop to record your total strokes after a hole?
   a. At the green you just finished
   b. At the tee of the following hole
   c. At the clubhouse

7. Which of these is a parkland-style golf course?
   a. Augusta National
   b. St. Andrews
   c. Shinnecock Hills

8. The late golf architect Alister MacKenzie said golfers should be able to play a true links course with just one club. Which club?
   a. 5-iron
   b. Pitching wedge
   c. Putter

9. What is the most famous target-style golf course?
   a. TPC at Sawgrass
   b. St. Andrews
   c. Chalk Mountain

10. Where does a golf hole begin?
    a. At the green
    b. At the fairway
    c. At the tee

Answers: 1. b; 2. b; 3. b; 4. c; 5. a; 6. b; 7. a; 8. c; 9. a; 10. c

STEP 3: RULES AND ETIQUETTE

ETIQUETTE

Etiquette is a word for good manners. Unlike some sports, golfers aren't supposed to bother their opponents or try to prevent them from playing well. In basketball, you do everything you can, within the rules, to keep your opponents from being successful. In golf, just the opposite is true – you do nothing to bother your opponent.

Indeed, you do all you can to make him or her comfortable. That's why you should stand still and be quiet while other golfers in your group hit. It's why you're supposed to stand far away from your opponent so he will not hit you or see you while he swings.

My basic rule of golf etiquette is similar to the Golden Rule: treat others as well, or better, than you want to be treated. I hope you'll take what I have to say now to heart. Be considerate of the golf course and the game's rules. Replace your divots, put garbage in a trash can, repair ball marks and play by the rules.

To learn the game's basic rules and etiquette, I suggest you purchase the official rulebook, the *Rules of Golf*.

Here are some basic tips for good golf etiquette.

1. Enter a bunker from the lowest point of the bunker. It's dangerous, and bad for the maintenance of the bunker, to enter from the highest side.
2. Be silent while somebody else is swinging.
3. If somebody else is putting, stand in a place where the player can't see you.
4. Gather information about your shot while other people are hitting so you will be ready to swing when it's your turn.
5. Pace of play is a very important part of good etiquette. Always keep up with the group ahead of you.
6. When putting, place your bag near, but not on, the green.
7. Before putting, set the flagstick down gently on the edge of the green.
8. Repair ball marks on the green with a ball-mark repair tool or a tee.
9. Replace divots. A divot is the chunk of grass you remove from the ground by hitting the ball.

RULES

There are two basic rules of golf: (1) play the ball as it lies and the course as you find it, and (2) on each hole, start at the tee and keep hitting the ball until it goes into the hole. That's everything.

If you can't play the ball as it lies or keep hitting it until it goes in the hole, there is a specific rule to govern the situation. You will find a specific rule to govern every conceivable situation in the *Rules of Golf*. The book has 34 rules and 150 pages. No matter how bizarre the ball's position, there's a rule to tell you what to do.

For example, if you shank a shot, and your ball hits a tree, bounces back and hits your foot, Rule 19-2 provides the unfortunate fact that you must take a 2-stroke penalty. Or, if you curve your ball wildly to the left, over the course boundary fence and into your friend's barbecue, Rule 27-1 governs this situation. (Look it up and see what you must do!)

Of the 34 rules in the *Rules of Golf*, golfers use only a few of them regularly, and the following rules are the ones I expect my juniors to know as well as they know how to add and subtract. The most important rules pertain to lost balls (Rule 27), balls that are out of bounds (Rule 27), definitions of and relief from obstructions (Rule 24), relief from abnormal ground conditions (Rule 25), when to play a provisional ball (Rule 27), relief from and types of water hazards (Rule 26) and the definition of a stroke (Definitions chapter, p.12).

IF THE PUTT'S 'GOOD', YOU'LL MAKE IT

When I was playing tournament golf for a living, I'd often miss short putts, also known as 'gimmes' or 'tap-ins'. One reason I missed so often was because as I approached short putts, I told myself that I had no chance to miss. When I stood over the putt, however, the putt was usually longer than it had appeared from far away. As a result, I was afraid that I might miss and I often did.

My mistake? Letting the distance of the putt determine my attitude.

Having learned this lesson about putting and concentration the hard way – missing short putts contributed to spoiling my career as a tour player – I wanted to make sure my students would focus 100 per cent over every shot. That's why, whenever a student hits his or her ball close to the hole and asks, 'Is the rest of this good?' I say, 'Take your time. If the putt is good, you won't miss it.'

STEP 3: QUIZ

1. Of the 80 million people 19 and under in the United States, how many of them play golf?
   a. 12 million
   b. 4 million
   c. 36 million

2. Who won the first US Women's Open, in 1946?
   a. Babe Zaharias
   b. Annika Sorenstam
   c. Patty Berg

3. Who won the first men's US Open, in 1895?
   a. 'Old Tom' Morris
   b. Horace Rawlins
   c. Walter Hagen

4. Which organisation publishes the *Rules of Golf*?
   a. PGA Tour
   b. United States Golf Association (USGA)
   c. LPGA

5. What is a mulligan?
   a. An extra chance to hit a shot
   b. A type of frog
   c. A water hazard

6. How many penalty strokes do you receive if your golf ball ricochets off a tree and hits you in the thigh?
   a. 2
   b. 0
   c. 1

7. What is the maximum number of clubs you can carry in your bag, according to the *Rules of Golf*?
   a. 11
   b. 20
   c. 14

8. How many golfers are there in the world?
   a. 800,000
   b. 60 million
   c. 1 billion

9. Which association is in charge of the biggest men's professional golf tour in the United States?
   a. PGA of America
   b. PGA Tour
   c. First Tee

10. What is the most severe penalty you can get for being late for your tee time in a tournament?
    a. 2 strokes
    b. 5 strokes
    c. Disqualification

Answers: 1. b; 2. c; 3. b; 4. b; 5. a; 6. a; 7. c; 8. b; 9. b; 10. c

STEP 4: HOW A GOLF COURSE OPERATES

WHEN TO PLAY

Golf courses are open from sunrise to sunset. Saturday mornings are the busiest times at private and public courses. If you're a beginner, avoid playing on Saturday mornings. You'll feel rushed and tense, and you won't be able to hit multiple shots from the same position. The next busiest times are Friday and Sunday mornings. The slowest times – and the time I suggest beginners play – are all day on Tuesdays and Thursdays, and late afternoons on any day.

My favourite time to play golf is at the end of the day, a few hours before sunset. This is called the 'twilight' time, and many courses offer discounted fees during this time period.

Most public facilities are open seven days a week. Many private clubs are closed one day a week, usually Monday.

STARTING TIMES AND HOW TO MAKE ONE

A starting time is an appointment to begin your round. It's the time at which you're scheduled to hit your first shot. If you have a 10:00 a.m. starting time, you and the other players in your group must be on the first tee hitting your first shots at precisely 10:00 a.m. You should arrive at the course at least 20 minutes before your starting time. If you want to warm up, arrive 45 minutes before the starting time.

Your starting time is not when you should walk into the pro shop to pay for the round, or when your parents should drop you off at the course.

In a tournament, you can be penalised for missing your starting time. I know, because it happened to me. In the mid-1980s, I was running a little late one morning before a tournament run by the Southern California PGA Section. About an hour before my tee time, I pulled off the freeway and called the tournament chairman to tell him that I might be late. He said, 'If you're more than five minutes late for your starting time, you'll be disqualified according to the rules. There's nothing I can do.' The official was referring to Rule 6-3, which says, 'The player shall start at the time laid down by the committee,' and the penalty for breaching the rule is disqualification. The tournament committee for that event had decided to allow a five-minute grace period for tee times, but I arrived at the first tee seven minutes late for my tee time, and as a result was disqualified.

At both private and public courses, you make a starting time by calling the course in advance and asking for the starter. Most courses take reservations at least seven days in advance. Some courses take starting times through the Internet. Usually, the starter works in the golf shop, but sometimes he or she has a separate office.

EVEN WHEN I WAS EARLY, I WAS LATE

Tiger didn't like it when I was late, and I must admit I was late a lot. If I was five minutes tardy to pick up Tiger to go and play, he was definitely bothered, even when he was a little boy. I always tried to be prompt when going to the Woodses' home, in Cypress, but I usually scheduled too many things on my calendar each day, and I always left for appointments at the very last minute.

After parking on the street in front of the Woodses' house, half blocking their driveway, I'd run up the footpath. Their two dogs were always barking. To shut them up, Tida would scream, 'It's Rudy! It's Rudy!' and they would calm down.

I didn't have to look at my watch to know that I was late. Tiger's serious expression would tell the story. He wouldn't get mad, but his look would say, 'C'mon Rudy, where've you been? Let's get going. We've got golfing to do!' Tiger, rightly so, would make me feel guilty for being late. After all, I was holding up his fun. By the time we would get on to the road to the course, though, Tiger had usually forgiven me, and he wouldn't stop talking about how excited he was about our upcoming round.

Eventually, I learned my lesson and started showing up early. On a morning when I was taking Tiger to see the Los Angeles Open, I had planned to meet Earl and Tiger for breakfast at the Holiday Inn in Pacific Palisades. Our appointment was for 9:00 a.m. I arrived at 8:15, sat down in a booth and had a cup of coffee. While I was waiting, Earl and Tiger arrived and sat down in the opposite side of the dining room, and we didn't see each other. At 9:00 a.m., I began looking around the restaurant for Earl and Tiger. When I found them, sitting at a table, Tiger gave me that look. I was late again.

HOW LONG A ROUND TAKES

If you maintain a proper pace, a foursome should take three and a half to four hours to play an 18-hole round. Unfortunately, golfers are often considerably slower. At my two courses, an average 18-hole round takes between four and a half and five hours during prime time. Playing alone, and with nobody else on the course, you could easily play 18 holes in less than three hours. I often find that the quicker I play, the better I play.

Some golfers have taken speed to an extreme, creating a form of golf called Xtreme (or speed) golf. Xtreme golfers wear running shoes and carry only a few clubs – a long or a mid-iron, a wedge and a putter. The best Xtreme golfers can play 18 holes in one hour and break 80.

PACE OF PLAY

There's only one rule about pace in golf: always keep up with the group in front of you. This rule has no exceptions. If you can't keep up with the group ahead, you should not be on the course. That's not a form of discrimination. It's the only way to make golf enjoyable for everybody on the course.

When you're on the first tee, you'll be waiting for the group ahead to either leave the green (on a par 3), reach the green (on a par 4) or hit their second shots (on a par 5). You need to remain this close to the group throughout the round.

Skill has nothing to do with pace. I know plenty of 100-plus shooters who comfortably play 18 holes, in groups of four, in less than three and a half hours. I also know plenty of 70-shooters who take over five hours to play 18 holes.

STEP 4: QUIZ

1. How many strokes does a golfer take on a hole when he or she makes a 'snowman'?
   a. 6
   b. 8
   c. 10

2. Which professional golfer used to wear sneakers during tournaments?
   a. Se Ri Pak
   b. David Duval
   c. Gabriel Hjertstedt

3. Who was Jack Grout?
   a. The founder of Augusta National Golf Club

   b. Jack Nicklaus's childhood golf instructor
   c. A commissioner of the LPGA Tour

4. What is the 'lumberyard'?
   a. The woods on a golf course
   b. Where you buy wood
   c. The practice tee

5. How long should it take a foursome to play 18 holes?
   a. 3 ½ to 4 hours
   b. 4 ½ to 5 hours
   c. 2 ½ to 3 hours

6. In which city in California did Tiger Woods grow up?
   a. Pebble Beach
   b. Cypress
   c. San Francisco

7. Which professional golfer grew up with a 25-yard par 3 hole in the backyard?
   a. Karrie Webb
   b. Sergio Garcia
   c. Phil Mickelson

8. What connects the clubhead to the grip?
   a. Shaft
   b. Grooves
   c. Loft

9. Who was the first man to win three consecutive professional major championships?
   a. Tiger Woods
   b. Ben Hogan
   c. Bobby Jones

10. What is the best place to enter a sand bunker?
    a. The lowest point of the edge
    b. Anywhere
    c. The point of the edge that's closest to the green

Answers: 1. b; 2. c; 3. b; 4. a; 5. a; 6. b; 7. c; 8. a; 9. b; 10. a

STEP 5: COOL STUFF ABOUT THE GAME

WHERE GOLF STARTED

Games similar to golf were played in the middle centuries of the second millennium, but the game we know as golf started in St Andrews, Scotland, approximately 260 years ago. That's when the first golfing clubs, then called societies, were formed in Scotland. Some of the first societies were the Royal Burgess Golfing Society of Edinburgh, the Honourable Company of Edinburgh Golfers, the Musselburgh Golf Society and the Society of St Andrews Golfers. The oldest major tournament is the British Open, which started in 1860 at Prestwick Golf Club in Scotland. The winner was Willie Park. Golf came to the United States in the middle of the nineteenth century. The first US Open was held in 1895 at the Newport (RI) Golf Club, and the champion was Horace Rawlins. Patty Berg won the first US Women's Open, held in 1946 at Spokane (WA) Country Club.

TYPES OF SHOTS

Golfers have given names to the different types of wayward shots. The shots are explained below for a right-handed golfer. Switch the directions if you're a left-hander.

Hook: A shot that curves a lot to the left.

Slice: A shot that curves a lot to the right.

Draw: A shot that curves a little to the left.

Fade: A shot that curves a little to the right.

Top: A shot that never gets in the air, but rolls or bounces along the ground.

Skull: A topped shot in which the leading edge of the clubface hits the middle of the ball. The ball flies out very low and fast, often along or just above the ground.

Sky ball: A shot that goes straight up towards the sky and travels considerably less distance than you had intended to hit it. A sky ball usually happens when the clubface slides under the ball, making contact with just a little bit of the bottom of the ball.

Pop-up: A mini sky ball.

HANDICAP

The golf handicap is a number that reflects your personal score if you play well. Handicaps are computed through a complex mathematical equation using the ten best 18-hole scores from your last 20 rounds, comparing the scores to the difficulty of the golf courses that you played. The difficulty of a course has two components: the rating and the slope.

FORMS OF COMPETITION

There are several different ways to keep score and compete while playing golf. The most common forms of competition are stroke play and match play. In stroke play, the player who hits the fewest shots wins; in match play, a round is divided into 18 separate matches, each hole being a stroke-play match. The person who wins the most holes, or matches, is the winner.

Most forms of competition are described in the *Rules of Golf*. Here are explanations of the most common competitions, besides match and stroke play.

Alternate shot: A team event with two-person teams. One team member tees off on even-numbered holes, and his or her partner tees off on odd-numbered holes. On each hole, the player who didn't tee off hits the second shot, and the teammates continue to alternate shots until the ball goes into the hole. You can use match- or stroke-play formats with alternate-shot play.

Bestball (also called fourball): A team event with two-person teams. Each player on a team hits her or his ball until it goes into the hole, and the lowest score of the two players counts for that team on each hole. Bestball can be used in match play or stroke play. In match play, you compete against another team on a hole by hole basis. In stroke play, you can compete against any number of teams.

Scramble: A team competition with two to five players on each team. Every player on a team tees off. The team captain then selects the best tee shot and everybody hits from that position. This process continues until the ball goes into the hole.

Stableford: A form of individual competition. Each player gets points based on his score for a hole relative to a fixed score or par. There are different Stableford point scales, but on each hole you always start at a fixed point, or par. For example, making the fixed point (e.g., 5 strokes on a par 5 hole), or a par, is usually worth 1 point. Anything over the fixed point, or par, is no points or minus points. If you score better than the fixed point, or par, you gain points.

The tournament committee predetermines the point system, and the winner is the competitor who accrues the most points. The Stableford system is used in a PGA Tour event called the International, held every summer since 1986 at Castle Pines Golf Club in Castle Rock, Colorado.

FITNESS
High-tech equipment is not the only reason professionals are hitting the ball longer than ever. You have to be in good condition to play your best golf. There are exceptions to the rule, but in order for most golfers to fulfil their potential, they need to be as strong and as healthy as possible. Stronger people hit the ball farther than weaker people; long is good and longer is better in golf.

EQUIPMENT

PARTS OF THE CLUB
Grip: The end of the club that is designed to be held. It's a tube-shaped piece of rubber – sometimes leather – attached to the end of the shaft that's opposite the clubhead. The grip absorbs most of the vibration caused by hitting the ball. Grips should be changed once a year if you're an avid player.
Shaft: A long and skinny tube made of steel or graphite (some are made of titanium and other exotic materials) that connects the clubhead to the grip.
Head: A little piece of metal (some are made of wood or graphite) which is about the size of an adult's fist and is designed for hitting the ball. Each head in a set of clubs has a

unique design to make the ball take off at a different launch angle. Head designs can also accommodate different 'lies', such as thick grass or sand. For example, some metal-wood heads have narrow rails across the bottom to help the club glide through thick grass.

Here are the most important parts of a clubhead.

- *Face*: The head's front side, which hits the ball.
- *Heel:* The lower corner of the head that is nearest to you while standing in the address position.
- *Hosel:* The socket in the head that is located just above the heel. The shaft fits into the clubhead through the hosel.
- *Sole:* The bottom edge of the clubhead. A club's number is often located on the sole.
- *Toe:* The lower corner of the head that is farthest from you while standing at address.

BALLS

There are two basic ball styles: wound and non-wound. Wound balls have a rubber core surrounded by a long, skinny strip of rubber, like a long rubber band. Non-wound balls have a solid core. Wound balls used to be the model of choice for top players because, despite the fact that they didn't go quite as far as non-wound models, they were softer than non-wound models and thus easier to control around the green. But wound balls are virtually obsolete, having been replaced by non-wound models that have soft covers.

That said, almost all golf balls are good. You have to be a very low handicapper for the ball to make any difference in your game. Even if you are an expert golfer, a golf ball will affect you more mentally than physically.

BAGS

Bags come in all sizes, but the only good golf bags are those that are light and easy to carry. Nobody needs a big bag. Most tour professionals carry enormous staff bags. Surprisingly, pros usually have fewer things packed in their bags than average golfers have in their much smaller bags. The pros use these enormous bags only because they get paid to use them. When pros play at home, they often use small, light bags. Several country clubs with caddies have banned oversize bags by setting weight limits.

SUNBLOCK
Please heed the following advice: in the summer months wear sunblock at all times on the golf course, even if it's cloudy. I recommend putting at least 30 SPF sunscreen on your arms, face, legs and neck whenever you play. Some courses offer free sunblock in the locker room or in the pro shop. If free sunblock isn't displayed, don't be shy about asking for it.

STEP 5: QUIZ
1. How old was Tiger Woods when he took his first golf lesson from Rudy Duran?
   a. 5 years old
   b. 4 years old
   c. 9 years old

2. What is the heaviest club?
   a. Driver
   b. Wedge
   c. 5-iron

3. What PGA Tour event uses the Stableford scoring system?
   a. Players Championship
   b. Byron Nelson Classic
   c. The International

4. Who's the first golfer to have owned a Gulfstream V, the world's most expensive private jet?
   a. Greg Norman
   b. Tiger Woods
   c. Arnold Palmer

5. What is a hook?
   a. A shot that curves a lot from right to left, for a right-hander
   b. A shot that curves a lot from left to right, for a right-hander
   c. A shot that curves a little from left to right, for a right-hander

6. What is a skull?
   a. A shot into the water
   b. A shot off the club's leading edge, which flies low and fast
   c. A shot off the toe

7. What's a 'fried egg'?
   a. A ball buried in wet turf
   b. A ball partially buried in a sand bunker
   c. A ball in a pile of rocks

8. What professional golfer's nickname is 'Boss of the Moss'?
   a. Phil Mickelson
   b. Annika Sorenstam
   c. Loren Roberts

9. What is 'duck soup'?
   a. A dirty pond
   b. A group of bad golfers
   c. A bad drive

10. What is golf's oldest major championship?
    a. Masters
    b. U.S. Women's Amateur
    c. British Open

Answers: 1. b; 2. b; 3. c; 4. a; 5. a; 6. b; 7. b; 8. c; 9. b; 10. c

9. GAMES
PLAYING GAMES WHILE YOU PRACTISE MAKES PRACTISING FUN

Some of the most fun in golf comes from playing games (as opposed to rounds) and participating in friendly competitions. Playing games is also an excellent way to improve. Many golf games are played away from the course, on places like the driving range, the putting green and even in a backyard.

My young students and I regularly compete against each other. We indulge in putting, chipping and long-driving contests. We also have competitions in which the winner is the person who creates the most sensational shot. For example, we'll see who can hit the highest ball with a driver, or who can hit the biggest hook with a sand wedge. One game involves trying to hit the individual numbers that are painted on yardage signs at the practice range.

Most golf fans, and even some TV commentators and Tour players, are awestruck when Tiger hits what looks like an impossible shot. I'm never (well, rarely) the least bit surprised at anything Tiger does on the golf course. What to the average golfer looks like a scary situation is, in fact, an opportunity to create a shot. It's a chance to adapt your shot-making skills to a new situation, and to succeed at something that nobody may have ever dreamed possible. That's fun and exciting, not scary. What's the worst that could happen? The shot doesn't work out the way you had planned. So what?

When Tiger hits an errant shot, spectators might cringe because it looks like Tiger is in trouble. But Tiger probably isn't fretting about his predicament. As he's walking to his ball, he's likely concocting a plan to hit his next shot. He's trying to recall instances in which he's hit similar shots, and, in many cases, those instances will be games that he played as a child.

When you're on the golf course, consider every situation as an opportunity to hit a perfect shot, whether your ball is in the middle of the fairway or in the middle of the woods. Playing with such a positive mindset is the only way to enjoy golf as much as you possibly can, and to play to the best of your ability.

Playing games will help you learn the nuances of shot making, and it will dispel the false notion that hitting a golf shot should be a fearful experience. Golf is fun, right? So what's up with being afraid? If playing games becomes part of your regular golfing experience, you'll find that your attitude on the course will be upgraded from an 'Uh oh, I hope I get over the trees' mindset to a 'Great, I'm going to whale this ball right over that tree and put it on the green' attitude.

Devote a portion of every practice session to hitting shots you've never tried. Try to hit high and soft chips with your 5-iron and low, curving screamers with your pitching wedge. Always hit to a target, whether it's a yard marker, a flagstick, a coloured patch of grass or a ball out on the range.

There is no limit to the creativity you can utilise when devising new games. Push the creativity envelope as far as you can, but don't disturb other golfers or break rules at the course. You'll know you've gone too far if you get in trouble with the golf course manager.

Although Tiger and I never got in trouble, we pushed the limits on more than one occasion at the Navy Course in Los Alamitos, California, where he and I practised frequently when he was a boy. In one game, we played through the hedges by the second tee, down the service road and back through the hedges to the tee. The winner was the person who played this routing in the fewest strokes.

You won't win every game you play, but that's not the point. Playing will develop your golf imagination, and that is as important as swing technique when it comes to shooting low scores. I've provided my favourite games in this chapter, but these games are only a minuscule number of the golf games that exist. There are also many games that don't yet exist, and perhaps you will be the person who creates them! There's one rule to follow when you create a game: the stranger and more challenging the game is, the more fun it will be to play.

MY FAVOURITE GAMES

1. THE FUN METER

Play an entire round without keeping track of the number of shots you hit on each hole. Instead, keep track of how many good shots you hit and how much fun you had on each hole. (Don't keep track of bad shots. Those should be deleted from your memory!)

On your scorecard, write two numbers in the little box that exists for each hole. On the left side of the box, write the number of good strokes you took on the hole. On the right side of the box, write a number that corresponds to how much fun you had. For grading your fun, 1 is the worst score (it means you had no fun) and 10 is the best score (you loved playing the hole).

Rating how much fun you have on a hole is a subjective process, and it's up to you to decide what makes a hole fun. Some ways of measuring fun include recalling how much you smiled on the hole, whether you were nice to your playing partners and whether you let your score affect your attitude.

This game, which I learned from Lynn Marriott, a golf instructor from Phoenix, is a terrific exercise because it emphasises fun – the number one reason we play golf – and it takes the focus off the number of times you hit the ball. Remember, allowing your happiness to be affected by your score is a sure-fire way to ensure that you will rarely enjoy playing golf. If you don't believe me, listen to this story about my friend Steve.

MY FRIEND FINALLY LEARNS THE POINT OF PLAYING GOLF: TO HAVE FUN!

Steve is in his mid-fifties. He's been playing golf since he was a teenager, and he has been a professional for over thirty years. Steve quit playing in tournaments for a living ten years ago to become the director of men's professional golf tours in Asia and South America.

Steve stopped working with the professional tours in the late 1990s and began thinking about returning to tournament golf. He wanted to qualify for the Senior PGA Tour, but he knew that his game was not good enough and that he needed help. Steve and I are good friends, and we occasionally talked about how he could improve.

The first thing I noticed about Steve after watching him hit balls on the practice tee was that his swing looked pretty good. He looked comfortable over the ball, and his best shots were definitely Senior Tour material. But Steve just wasn't having any fun at the course.

After about ten minutes, I asked Steve a difficult question. 'Have you ever had any fun playing golf?'

I could tell the question surprised Steve because his eyes suddenly perked up. He stood tall and silent. I could feel tension in the air, as if I'd brought up a topic that Steve had been hiding in the back of his mind for a long time. After what seemed like a couple hours – but was actually a couple of minutes – Steve admitted, 'You know, Rudy, I don't remember having much fun playing golf.'

Steve looked like a different person after saying that. It was as if he had just discovered something about himself that he'd never let himself admit. I enquired more about the stunning admission. 'You didn't even have fun when you were a star on your high school golf team?'

'No, I didn't have much fun then either,' Steve said. 'I only felt good when I won a match or played well, but that certainly wasn't all the time.'

Here was a man who had been shooting in the 70s since school, and who, as a professional, had won thousands of dollars in prize money and several tournaments over a long career. Still, he'd hardly had any fun. Steve and I had several long talks about his future in golf. He decided that his real problem wasn't his swing, as he had previously thought, but his attitude. Steve finally understood that he had spent decades trying to improve his swing mechanics and relating his self-worth to his golf scores.

Steve said that he wanted to make golf fun. We both felt that doing that would make him feel a lot better, and his scores would probably go down too.

The new attitude made a huge difference. He didn't attempt to play on the Senior Tour, but he went into the golf-club exporting business, which allows him enough time to compete occasionally in tournaments. When Steve plays golf now, he tells me what he enjoys about his time on the course. Not every round is a joyful experience, but he is having infinitely more fun at golf today than he ever did, and he is working diligently to reach the point where every day on the golf course is a great day.

2. PUTT PUTT

This game is for two to six people. On the practice putting green, play nine to 18 different holes. Sometimes my students play up to 54 holes in one game. The winner is the player who takes the lowest number of strokes combined for all the holes. On a sunny day, the putting greens at my courses are full of people playing Putt Putt, often until the sun goes down, and sometimes after it has already set. You can use the stroke- or match-play format.

You can also play Putt Putt with teams. Each team takes the best score from among its players, or you can count everybody's score, coming up with a total team score for each hole.

The rules are simple. You have to put the ball into the hole on every green, and there are no gimmes. Everybody has to hole out on every hole. Never pick up your ball unless you're retrieving it from the bottom of the hole.

You can designate a course before starting to play, or the person (or team) that has the honour selects the hole. Be sure to play lots of different holes, mixing up short and long ones, uphillers and downhillers, putts with lots of curve and others that are flat and straight.

3. ROW PUTTING

This game is for two or more competitors. Each player brings one ball and his putter to the practice green. Pick a spot between 4 and 8 feet from the hole, and mark the spot with a tee. The winner is the person who can make the greatest number of consecutive putts from the spot.

You can vary this game by predetermining the number of putts each person will take, in which case the winner is the player who makes the most putts out of the preset number.

Lots of tour pros play this game alone, when they have nobody to practise with. When Annika Sorenstam plays this game, she doesn't quit until she has made 100 in a row. Sometimes she ends up putting under moonlight!

4. CHIP-N-PUTT
This game provides chipping and putting practice, and highlights the need to chip close to the hole so you can one-putt. You can play alone, or in a group. Each participant chips to a hole from a position near the green. You get 5 points if your ball goes directly into the hole; 1 point if you take one chip and one-putt to get into the cup; and minus 1 point if you chip and take two or more putts to hole out. You can play one-putt up to a fixed number of points, or for a predetermined amount of time or number of holes.

5. UNCLE
You play with two people, one hole at a time, determining the winner of each hole either by total strokes or whoever makes a hole-in-one. (If both people make a hole-in-one, it's a tie.) You continue playing until somebody gets so far ahead that the other player gives up, saying, 'Uncle'. Although most people play this game one on one, you can play with up to four people. You can select the holes that you'll play before starting, but I don't think that's as fun as making up the holes along the way.

6. TWO- OR THREE-CLUB GOLF
This is one of the most fun and helpful games. It also provides a wonderful education about golf's intangibles. Play a round with only three clubs: a 5-iron, a wedge and a putter. You can substitute different clubs for the ones I recommend.

Surprisingly, your scores probably won't be much higher for rounds in which you use only a few clubs than for the rounds in which you use a full set. In some cases, you'll even shoot lower with only a few clubs, because having a few clubs takes the pressure off and negates indecision. Selecting a club for a 140-yard approach will be easy. You'll use the only club you can – the mid-iron. You'll also learn to focus more on feel than on technique, because you have to hit a single club many different distances. For example, you'll learn how to hit a 5-iron from the position that you'd normally use an 8-iron, and doing that requires a shorter swing than you usually use.

I once shared this drill with a 3-handicapper who had reached a wall in his quest to improve. The problem, he told me, was that he felt too anxious over every shot, even from the middle of the fairway. I suggested that he try playing with only a few clubs in his bag. A couple of weeks later, the man told me that he had played almost as well with three clubs as he had been playing with his whole set, and that the drill had opened a new window on golf. He had learned to appreciate golf not so much as a quest for technical perfection or a score, but as a fun game filled with opportunities to hit different shots.

Moe Norman, the legendary player and teacher from Canada, always talked about the absolute necessity of varying our routines on the golf course. I heard Moe talk when I played the Canadian tour in the 1970s. One of Moe's favourite theories was that you could play a short par 4 by hitting a wedge and then a driver as easily as you could by hitting a driver followed by a wedge. Moe proved his point by making a par hitting a wedge and then a driver to reach the green or holes during actual rounds.

7. CHIP AND PUTT WITHOUT A PUTTER

This game has the same rules as chip-n-putt, with one exception. You have to hit every shot with a club other than the putter. You can putt with any club you like, and it doesn't have to be the same club you chip with. Putting with a club different from your putter will help to improve your feel. After playing this game a few times, you will discover that you can putt well without a putter.

8. TEE GAMES

Trash can: On a busy day you often have to wait on the tee, and it's fun to play games while waiting. One of my favourite games to play on the tee is to pitch a ball into a trash can. This game has two variations. In one, the winner is the first to make it into the can in one shot. You can also play so the winner is the person who takes the fewest strokes to hit his ball into the can.

In a variation of the trash can game, you pitch the ball at the trash can while standing close to the can, and the winner is the person who makes it into the can in one shot from the closest distance.

Shooting gallery: Other games to play on the tee include trying to bounce the ball off the top of a bench or other objects. You can also take a cup out of the trash, put a ball in the bottom of the cup, set the cup on the bench and try to knock the cup off the bench. I call this the shooting gallery game. One warning: don't stand behind the bench while your friends fire at the cup.

Hit the mark: It's also fun to try to hit tee markers from a few yards away with different clubs.

Over the mark: Tiger and I played a game involving the tee signs that have information about the hole. The goal of the game was to see who could stand as close to the sign as possible and still hit his ball up and over the sign. To do this, you have to swing as hard as you can and try sliding the club directly under the ball, popping it straight up.

9. IN OR OUT

Play this game on the practice tee, hitting shots to a defined target area. Select left and right side boundaries, using yardage marker signs, flagsticks or other objects that are on the range.

This game is good for one or more players. Each person gets a predetermined number of balls. If you have more than one person, take turns hitting, with each player getting two or three shots per round. The winner is the person who hits the most shots that stop within the predetermined boundaries.

You can add a distance minimum or maximum to this game. For example, you can determine that a shot will only count as a winner if it stops within the boundaries and travels a minimum or a maximum distance.

10. TARGET PRACTICE

Select a target on the driving range. The target could be a flagstick, a yardage sign or a discoloured patch of turf. Each player gets 18 balls, and you play the game in nine rounds, with each player hitting two shots per round. The closest ball to the target wins each round, and the champion has the most winning rounds out of nine. You can vary the number of balls and rounds.

You can also be creative and determine that a shot must take no more than three bounces before it stops rolling. You can also make specific shot requirements, such as saying that a shot only qualifies if it curves from right to left, or does not fly higher than 30 feet. When you add specific flight requirements, it's good to have one person sit out the game and be the judge, objectively determining whether a shot meets the requirements.

11. 7-UP

This is a putting game in which the first person to 7 points wins. You play to a predetermined hole on the practice green, or the winner of each hole selects the following hole. You earn 3 points for a one-putt and 1 point for a two-putt, and you lose 3 points for a three-putt or worse. Senior tour player Don Pooley is a fan of this game, and he is one of the best putters in the history of golf. In fact, Pooley was the PGA Tour's top-ranked putter in 1988 and 1997.

12. SINKS

A sink is a one-putt, and in this game you get 1 point for a sink. There's no other way to score a point, and you never lose points because you pick up your ball if you don't make it into the hole with your first try. Play with any number of competitors and up to a predetermined number of points.

10. CLUB FITTING
YOU CAN PLAY YOUR BEST ONLY IF YOUR CLUBS FIT

I'd be rich if I had a dollar for every golfer I have seen using improperly fitted clubs, and that's a shame. It's nearly impossible to develop a good swing if your clubs are too big or too small. Just try playing with clubs that reach up to the middle of your chest or are so short you have to stoop down at address. You will make contact using poorly fitted clubs, but you probably won't shoot as low as you could with properly fitted equipment.

Age and sex are not, as many people believe, the determining factors in club fitting. In fact, age and sex have absolutely nothing to do with club fitting. The only way to determine the proper club specifications are to measure a player's size and strength (often measured in swing speed), and use those figures to select clubs. To get fitted, you should visit a golf professional or an expert club fitter. Nobody else has the necessary expertise to select clubs that will be tailor-made for you.

Club fitting has become popular in the last decade. You should not have to pay a fee for fitting if you purchase equipment from the same place that does your fitting. Golf clubs, driving ranges and speciality golf shops are the best places to get fitted. You can't get fitted over the Internet, no matter what a website claims. It's OK to purchase clubs through the Internet, but you should only do that if you know what your fitting 'specs' are.

Until recently, golf equipment makers put virtually all of their design efforts into building clubs for large adult (or male) body types. That left a lot of neglected golfers, mostly women and children, who had to use clubs that were not nearly as carefully designed. Recently, though, the golf industry has discovered that there is a significant number of women and children golfers, and to lure these people to buy their clubs, the companies have begun designing gear specifically for them.

Club fitters have also made progress, learning how to fit people of all shapes and sizes.

HOW I LEARNED THE VALUE OF CLUB FITTING

Because there was so little information about fitting women, children and small adults, I invented a special club-fitting system for those people twenty years ago. I've actually been fitting golfers for my entire career as a golf professional, which began in 1971. Back then hardly anybody knew anything about lub fitting. One of the few fitting experts in the country happened to be my first boss in the golf business, Al Wagner. Al owned a driving range in Studio City, California, when I was a teenager living in a nearby town named Sun Valley. In the summer of 1966, my senior year at Polytechnic High, Al gave me a job at his range that included basic maintenance chores and driving the ball retriever.

I joined the US Air Force as an airman in 1968 and was sent to a base in Topeka, Kansas. I took up golf in earnest in Topeka and, soon after arriving, earned a spot on the base golf team. I was honourably discharged from the Air Force as a sergeant in January 1971, by which time I had lowered my handicap to 3.

After leaving the military, I decided to pursue a career in golf for four reasons. First, I wanted to try to become a tour pro. Secondly, Al had strongly encouraged me to follow him into the business. By 1971, Al owned the Hasley Canyon Golf Course in Saugus and a small golf club company, and he wanted me to work for him. Thirdly, I wanted to provide children with the opportunities to learn and play the game that I didn't have while growing up. Finally, I believed that being a club professional and teacher would make me a better player. How was a naïve twenty-something like myself supposed to know the great irony of the golf profession: club pros rarely play golf!

While working for Al, my duties included working at his range, his course and his club company, which today is called Diamondhead Golf and is based in Sacramento, California. Working for Al is where I got my first exposure to club building, and I loved the handiwork.

In the spring of 1972, I took my club-fitting expertise and left Al to become an assistant pro at Heartwell Golf Park, a par 3 layout in Long Beach, California. Although I taught hundreds of kids at Heartwell in the 1970s, I didn't do too much club fitting for my pupils, because most of the kids in my junior programme were teenagers and already had clubs. What's more, the students who didn't have clubs were big enough so they didn't need cut-down clubs.

A FITTING REVELATION

My attitude towards club fitting changed, though, when a four-year-old Tiger Woods strolled into my shop in 1980. I was about to learn that I'd been making a huge mistake for years, because I had been using one set of fitting measurements to fit all golfers, regardless of their size.

Tiger already had a few clubs that had been cut down by his father, Earl. His set included a 2½-wood, a 7-iron and a putter. After giving him a few private lessons, it was obvious that Tiger was so skilled that he, unlike most kids his size and age, could benefit from having a sand wedge to learn the nuances of the short game. I found a bargain-barrel wedge for Tiger right away, and cut the club down using the standard club-fitting system I had been using for years.

The longest wood is always a driver, and the longest iron is a 1-iron. According to the standard system back then, each wood and each iron down the line from the driver and 1-iron, respectively, would be ½ inch smaller. So the 2-wood would be ½ inch shorter than the driver, the 3-wood would be ½ inch shorter than the 2-wood, and a 2-iron would be ½ inch shorter than a 1-iron. This method was carried throughout the set, all the way to the 5-wood and sand wedge, typically the shortest clubs in the bag.

Using this methodology, I calculated the length of what Tiger's sand wedge should be and cut down the club. But there was a problem. The wedge was far too short, even for Tiger, who was only 3ft 6in tall. Why didn't the wedge fit Tiger?

After racking my brain, the answer dawned on me. Tiger's driver was half the length of a standard driver, so the distance between each club in his set needed to be half the length of the distance between clubs in a standard set. Translation: make each club in Tiger's set ¼ inch shorter than the previous club, not ½ inch. Two decades later, this revelation seems obvious, but it was anything but that at the time.

Once I had made this adjustment, from ½ inch to ¼ inch per club, I cut down another bargain-barrel sand wedge for Tiger. This wedge, two inches longer than the previous club, fitted perfectly.

My experience with Tiger's wedge taught me that I needed to use a different formula from what the industry was prescribing if I wanted my smallest pupils to have properly fitted clubs. I determined that the formula should be based on the relationship between a player's driver and a standard-length driver. For example, if a girl needed a driver that was 75 per cent as long as a standard club, I would shorten all her clubs by 75 per cent of the adult standard of ½ inch per club, or ⅜ inch per club. This concept became the basic guideline for all my club fitting for juniors and smaller people.

This discovery inspired me to develop a club-fitting system for kids, which I call the Quik Fit System (see page 153). The Quik Fit allowed me to fit people instantly because it has club lengths predetermined for people of all sizes.

Quik Fit has eight sizes of clubs, the smallest based on a 27-inch driver and the longest on a 47-inch driver. The driver is the baseline club for club fitting, which, as I mentioned, determines the length of the rest of the clubs in your bag. To set the proper length for your driver, stand erect and let your arms hang loosely and naturally. The distance from the bottom of your elbow – either elbow is OK – to the ground is the measurement I use to determine the length of all a student's clubs.

To fit your child or yourself, use a measuring tape to determine the distance from your elbow or your child's elbow to the ground. Take that distance and find which of the eight categories it fits into. For example, a distance of 30 inches falls into the blue category, which is 73 per cent of a standard adult club. That would make for a ⅜-inch difference between clubs, and the chart provides shaft lengths for every club in the bag, including the putter.

My system was designed for cutting down clubs, but the measurements can be just as helpful if you're buying new clubs. Simply find which of the eight categories you or your child fits into, and make sure each club in the set you purchase is the same length as those in my chart.

Here are some answers to questions I'm commonly asked about club fitting.

● I have a five-year-old child. Can I get her pre-made clubs that I don't have to cut down?

Yes. Several companies produce clubs for all sizes of people. But don't rely solely on the size information the clubmakers provide. Ask the company to give you the length of each club you're buying, and compare the lengths to those in my Quik Fit system. The lengths don't need to match exactly, but they should be close.

● I bought my child a new set of clubs when he was five years old. Now he's seven and the clubs are too short. Can I have longer shafts attached to the old clubheads?

Yes, you can have new shafts attached to old clubheads. However, I recommend getting all new clubs, because the cost of reshafting a few junior clubs is almost always going to be comparable to the cost of buying new clubs. Most pro shops, especially those that are affiliated with a junior programme, are likely to take your child's old clubs as a trade-in, which will reduce the cost of new clubs. What's more, your trade-in set will provide an inexpensive opportunity for another child to get started in golf.

● How much should new clubs cost?

A new set of nine irons, three woods and a putter can cost as little as £250. That price doesn't include a bag, balls or other items. However, most kids don't need a full set of clubs. Junior sets, which typically include three or four irons, a wood, a putter and a bag, typically start at £75.

● **What'll happen if my child uses clubs that don't fit?**
It's possible to hit good shots with clubs that are too big or too small. But if a child grows up playing with improperly fitted clubs, he'll probably develop an incorrect address position and swing motion to compensate for the too-long or too-short clubs, and correcting the mechanical flaws will be difficult later in his career. That's why you must take the time to get the right clubs at the beginning of his career so you can imprint the proper motion.

KIDS CAN HIT 1-IRONS

When Tiger was five years old, I fitted him for his first full set of irons to replace his mixed-and-matched set of irons. We got the new sticks from Confidence Golf, in Gardena, California, because Earl and I knew Al Bernstein, a salesman at the company. Al was happy to custom-build a set to Tiger's personal specifications.

Tida, Tiger and I went to the factory so Tiger could select the clubheads he liked. The set he chose included a 3-iron through to a sand wedge. On the way home from the factory, Tiger matter-of-factly asked, 'Rudy, how come we didn't order a one- and a two-iron?'

I told Tiger that he didn't generate enough clubhead speed to use those clubs effectively. He didn't reply, but just looked at me quietly and thought about my answer. I thought that was the end of the story.

A week later, during a practice session at Heartwell, Tiger's dad was hitting balls on the range near us. He had a 1- and a 2-iron in his bag. In the middle of our lesson, Tiger excused himself for a moment, walked over to his dad's bag and grabbed his Ping Eye2 1-iron, which reached up to Tiger's neck. Tiger came back to our working area and striped a handful of shots with his dad's 1-iron, with the balls teed up. Tiger wasn't showing off. He was talking with his sticks, letting his dad and me know that he could hit a 1-iron and 2-iron, and that the clubs should therefore be in his set. The following day I called Al and added a 1-iron and a 2-iron to Tiger's set.

RUDY DURAN'S QUIK FIT CHART

	R&W STRIPE	B&W STRIPE	ORANGE	GREEN	BLACK	BLUE	WHITE	RED
% of adult male students	105%	100%	93%	85%	80%	73%	66%	60%
Difference in length between clubs, elbow to ground	9/16"	1/2"	7/16"	7/16"	3/8"	3/8"	5/16"	5/16"
	47" and up	41–46"	38–40"	35–37"	32–34"	29–31"	26–28"	23–25"
1 wood	47	45	42	39	36	33	30	27
3 wood	$45\frac{1}{8}$	44	$41\frac{1}{8}$	39	36	33	30	27
5 wood	$44\frac{3}{4}$	43	$40\frac{1}{4}$	$38\frac{1}{8}$	$35\frac{1}{4}$	$32\frac{1}{4}$	$29\frac{3}{8}$	27
7 wood	$43\frac{7}{8}$	42	$39\frac{3}{8}$	$37\frac{1}{4}$	$34\frac{1}{2}$	$31\frac{1}{2}$	$28\frac{3}{4}$	$26\frac{3}{8}$
9 wood	$42\frac{1}{2}$	41	$38\frac{1}{2}$	$36\frac{3}{8}$	$33\frac{3}{4}$	$30\frac{3}{4}$	$28\frac{1}{8}$	$25\frac{3}{4}$
2 iron	41	39	$36\frac{1}{4}$	$33\frac{3}{8}$	$31\frac{1}{4}$	$28\frac{1}{2}$	$25\frac{3}{4}$	$23\frac{1}{2}$
3 iron	$40\frac{7}{16}$	$38\frac{1}{2}$	$35\frac{13}{16}$	$32\frac{11}{16}$	$30\frac{7}{8}$	$28\frac{1}{8}$	$25\frac{7}{16}$	$23\frac{3}{16}$
4 iron	$39\frac{7}{8}$	38	$35\frac{3}{8}$	$32\frac{1}{4}$	$30\frac{1}{2}$	$27\frac{3}{4}$	$25\frac{5}{8}$	$22\frac{7}{8}$
5 iron	$39\frac{5}{16}$	$37\frac{1}{2}$	$34\frac{1}{2}$	$31\frac{3}{8}$	$29\frac{3}{4}$	27	$24\frac{1}{2}$	$22\frac{1}{4}$
6 iron	$38\frac{3}{4}$	37	$34\frac{1}{2}$	$31\frac{3}{8}$	$29\frac{3}{4}$	27	$24\frac{1}{2}$	$22\frac{1}{4}$
7 iron	$38\frac{3}{16}$	$36\frac{1}{2}$	$34\frac{1}{16}$	$30\frac{15}{16}$	$29\frac{3}{8}$	$26\frac{7}{8}$	$24\frac{3}{16}$	$21\frac{15}{16}$
8 iron	$37\frac{7}{8}$	36	$33\frac{3}{8}$	$30\frac{1}{2}$	29	$26\frac{1}{4}$	$23\frac{7}{8}$	$21\frac{15}{16}$
9 iron	$37\frac{1}{16}$	$35\frac{1}{2}$	$33\frac{3}{16}$	$30\frac{1}{16}$	$28\frac{7}{8}$	$25\frac{7}{8}$	$23\frac{9}{16}$	$21\frac{9}{16}$
P wedge	$36\frac{1}{2}$	35	$32\frac{3}{4}$	$29\frac{7}{8}$	$28\frac{1}{4}$	$25\frac{1}{2}$	$23\frac{1}{4}$	21
S wedge	$36\frac{1}{2}$	35	$32\frac{1}{4}$	$29\frac{7}{8}$	$28\frac{1}{4}$	$25\frac{1}{2}$	$23\frac{1}{4}$	21
Putter	$36\frac{1}{2}$	35	$32\frac{1}{4}$	$29\frac{7}{8}$	$28\frac{1}{4}$	$25\frac{1}{2}$	$23\frac{1}{4}$	21

Source: The Official Rules of Golf

11. PAR
WHAT IT IS, WHAT IT ISN'T AND HOW TO USE IT

When Tiger was five years old, his longest shot went about 100 yards. At best, he needed two shots to reach the green on a par 3, three shots to reach a par 4 and four shots to hit a par 5. Not being able to reach the greens in regulation meant that Tiger had virtually no chance of shooting par, but he was definitely *skilled* enough to shoot par.

To compensate for Tiger's lack of length, I devised a new scoring system tailored specifically for him. The system, which allowed him to have his own 'personal par', included par values that were higher than the standard pars on each hole. His personal par on a standard par 4, depending on its length, ranged from 5 to 7, and for 18 holes his par was around 90. At Heartwell Park, the par 3 course at which I was teaching, the par was 54 and Tiger's personal par at age five was 67.

Tiger has fired plenty of spectacular rounds as a professional, and a few years ago he shot a 13 under 59 during a practice round at his home course, Isleworth Golf Club in Windermere, Florida. However, I saw him play some of what I feel are his most impressive rounds when he was a child. Indeed, Tiger regularly bettered his personal par at Heartwell almost as soon as he began playing there. He would reach the greens on holes under 100 yards in one shot; on the other holes he needed to hit a driver and an iron to get to the green.

In March 1981, when Tiger was five, he made a par (based on his personal par) on the first hole at Heartwell and a birdie on the second hole, and after nine holes was 3-under par. On the back nine, he birdied the tenth hole, and at 13 – difficult hole for him because it was 130 yards long and he needed a driver and a good wedge to get home – he hit a drive and a wedge, and drained a birdie putt. Tiger was 5 under through 13 holes. I sensed that he was in the middle of a special round.

Indeed, he was. Tiger finished with an 8-under 59, and I could hardly believe it. He didn't mishit a single shot, and he made virtually every putt. He played with the composure of a seasoned tour pro, but he was only five years old. *Five!* The 59, to say the least, mightily impressed me. But Tiger wasn't all that impressed. To him, it was just another round. He figured that he should play like that all the time. Within a few years, he was breaking standard par at Heartwell.

WHAT IS PAR?

Most people think they know what par is, but when you ask them to explain it, they can't do it. Most golfers think par is the score for a hole, as provided on the scorecard, that everybody should make.

The par that's written on the scorecard is the score that an *expert* golfer would make if, as the *Rules of Golf* says, he or she has 'errorless play without flukes and under ordinary weather conditions, allowing two strokes on the putting green'. In layman's terms, that means par is what an expert would make if, in good weather, he or she plays a hole perfectly from tee to green and takes two putts.

In addition to indicating what an expert would make on a hole, the word *par* also represents the approximate distance of each hole. There are three measurement categories of par for men and four categories of par for women. These are based on distance. For example, a hole with a par of 3 is under 250 yards for men and under 210 yards for women. A par 72 course is probably going to be longer than a par 68 course.

The table opposite gives the different pars for men and women, according to the *Rules of Golf*.

Unless you're an expert golfer, par is a relative number that you should use solely to get a feel for the approximate length of a hole or a course. So if a hole is a par 3, that doesn't mean you should expect to take three strokes to put the ball into the hole. Rather, you should expect the hole to be 250 yards or less if you're a man, and 210 yards or less if you're a woman.

Non-expert golfers usually make the mistake of using standard par as a baseline to determine how well they have

PAR	MEN	WOMEN
3	Up to 250 yards	Up to 210 yards
4	251–470 yards	211–400 yards
5	471 yards and over	401–575 yards
6	No par 6 for men	576 and over yards

Source: The Official Rules of Golf

played a hole, or what they should expect to score for a hole or a round. Making that mistake causes far too many people to walk off the course feeling bad because their score is above standard par. In fact, they probably should feel good because their score was likely much better relative to par appropriate to their skill level.

Here's an example. A female 24-handicapper shoots 96 at a moderately difficult, par 71 course. She leaves the 18th green with a frown, ruminating over all the putts she missed. She thinks, 'I shot 25 over par and that stinks! Karrie Webb would have shot ten under par.' The fact is, this woman played well considering her skill level. She probably hit several excellent shots and should be pleased. She may aspire to shoot lower scores, but at this stage of her career she's not capable of shooting lower scores on a regular basis. The only way the woman could have broken 90 would have been to have had a career day.

If you're not an expert, and you want to compare your scores to an objective standard, you should use the junior par and personal par systems that I present on the following pages of this chapter. These two systems provide par ratings that have been created specifically for non-expert skill and distance levels.

The standard par system is useful, especially for professional and top-level amateur players and the competitions in which they participate. But standard par has, unfortunately, also become the measuring stick for players of average skill level, which is too bad. I have never used the standard par system, or any other par system, when scoring the weekly competitions in my junior programme. Instead, I divide the fields by age group, and the lowest score in each level wins. I never write anything about par on the scoreboard or tell kids their scores in relation to par, and the kids never ask. That keeps their thought focused on the only thing that's important: shooting the lowest score possible, regardless of any other factors, including par.

JOHN REVOLTA'S PAR-FECT REVELATION

I learned about personal par in the mid 1970s, when I began taking lessons from John Revolta. A Hall of Famer, Revolta won the 1935 PGA Championship and 17 other PGA Tour events. After retiring from competition he became one of the most famous teachers in the country, and he was especially noted for helping tour players, which is why I took lessons from him. I wasn't on the PGA Tour, but I wanted to be there, and I thought that John was the best person to help me achieve my dream.

John taught at Mission Hills Country Club in Rancho Mirage, California, and I frequently drove east from Long Beach to see him. During one of our first sessions, I told John about a terrible score I had made on a long par 4 at Mission Hills. On the hole, I had hit a decent drive down the fairway, but I was left with a 200-yard shot to a green which is protected by several bunkers and partially surrounded by water. Of course, my approach shot splashed into the drink.

John told me that I was crazy to have tried to reach the green. Instead, he suggested that I should have approached the hole as a par 5, laying up my second shot short of the water and bunkers instead of going for the green. I then could have pitched on to the putting surface, and I would have had a chance to make a 4. If I missed the putt, I would still have made 5, which is a good score on the hole. That strategy, which John called 'Your par,' would have turned a frustrating hole into a relatively easy and very fun hole. Playing the hole as a par 5 instead of a par 4 would have totally changed my expectations, and I would have been much more relaxed.

On the next two occasions I played the hole I took John's advice, buried my ego, and told myself that the hole was an easy par 5. The water no longer worried me because hitting a 40-yard approach over it, from the fairway to the green, was a simple shot. Guess what? I made stress-free 4s both times I played the hole. I used this new understanding of par everywhere, and I began playing significantly better.

Changing my expectations for the hole had freed up my mind and allowed me to play golf with a positive instead of a negative attitude. The change of thought lowered my score and, more important, helped me enjoy the round much more than I would have if I hadn't spoken to John.

That experience was a major revelation in my career, radically altering my perspective. Previously, I had considered golf to be frustrating and almost impossible to play well and enjoy. Now I began to see the game in a fresh light. I began evaluating holes and courses based on my skill level, not on the skill level that I thought I should have. It was a humbling but uplifting experience.

Ever since John gave me that invaluable advice, I've never paid attention to what the scorecard says about par when I play or when I evaluate other players' performances. You should think about par exactly like John taught me: forget about standard par, and think only about your personal par.

WHICH PAR SYSTEM IS RIGHT FOR YOU?

There are two individual par systems. The first is a skill-based system called skill-based par. The second is a distance-based system called personal par.

Skill-based par is a system that I created by modifying the junior par system, which was created by the United States Golf Association (USGA). My skill-based par system assigns par values to holes depending on your skill level and a hole's length.

Personal par is appropriate for advanced players who don't hit the ball far enough to reach standard-length holes in regulation and thus shouldn't use the standard par system.

Personal par was appropriate for Tiger because it is a distance-based system. He hit perfect shots almost all the time as a five-year-old, but he needed more strokes to reach the green than most adults. So he needed to establish a personal par that was based on his individual shot lengths. For example, an uphill 447-yard hole that was a par 4 on the scorecard would have been a par 7 or 8 in Tiger's personal par system.

To determine which par system you should use, first identify your skill level. There are three skill levels – beginner, intermediate and expert. Determining your level has nothing to do with how long you've been playing golf, and it's not an exact science. Beginners and intermediates should use the skill-based system, while experts should use the personal par system.

Here are some general guidelines.

1. **Beginner:** Has difficulty making solid contact.
2. **Intermediate:** Has some control in every discipline of the game, but he or she still makes lots of naïve mistakes.
3. **Expert:** Can control his or her golf ball and doesn't make many silly mistakes.

SKILL-BASED PAR

My skill-based par system has two levels, beginner and intermediate. To determine your par on a hole, first determine your skill level. Then, with the hole's yardage, determine what par value that yardage corresponds to at your skill level on my chart. For example, if you're a beginner and the first hole at your course is 328 yards long, the par for the hole would be 8.

Before starting to play, determine the par for each hole on the course and write those par values on your scorecard. Doing that will give you a realistic number of strokes you should try to score on each hole and for the entire round.

To use the skill-based par system, you'll need either to modify your course's scorecard or create a new scorecard from scratch.

PERSONAL PAR

Personal par is best-suited to golfers who can't hit the ball far enough to make regular pars. For example, personal par would be an ideal system for an 80-year-old man who is a great

PAR	BEGINNER	PAR	INTERMEDIATE
4	95 yards and less	3	145 yards and less
5	96–170 yards	4	146–260 yards
6	171–245 yards	5	261–370 yards
7	246–320 yards	6	371–490 yards
8	321–395 yards	7	491–525 yards
9	396–470 yards	8	526 yards and over
10	471 yards and over		

ball-striker but lacks strength, and thus can't hit the ball farther than 180 yards. Standard men's par won't provide him with realistic scores to aim for. On a 240-yard hole that is a par 3 for men, many older men won't be able to reach the green in one shot unless they bounce the ball off a rock or cartpath. So a 240-yard hole should be a par 4 for the 80-year-old man, because he has to hit a drive and a pitch to reach the green.

Personal par isn't designed for sharing among players, because everybody hits different distances. Personal par is something that you should keep to yourself; the par values you determine will be specific to your distance and skill levels.

You should not use a single set of personal pars forever. Rather, you should adjust your personal par daily, sometimes from hole to hole, depending on the weather. For example, I play with a personal par of 5 on the 450-yard par 4 seventh hole at San Luis Obispo Country Club – my home course – when I play the hole into the wind. When the hole plays downwind, however, it is significantly easier, and I use a personal par of 4.

Perhaps it seems like you need to do a lot of calculating while you play golf, but there's no other way to play with an accurate and realistic par value. Even the world's best players use personal par when they're in tournaments as important as the US Open. Shooting low scores requires mental discipline as much as it does good technique. It requires you to be constantly aware of your surroundings. If a hole is playing especially difficult, you need to re-evaluate what you can expect to score because golfing with unrealistic expectations is detrimental to playing your best.

Ben Hogan was in the habit of constantly adjusting his personal par depending on weather and course conditions. He did this famously on the 11th hole at Augusta National during the Masters. The green on the downhill par 4 has a lake adjacent to the left side of it, so Hogan always played safe, hitting his long-iron approach to a grassy collection area to the right. 'If you ever see me on the green,' Hogan once said about how he played the hole, 'you'll know I missed my second shot.'

Sometimes personal par makes holes easier than they are rated on the scorecard. A tour pro might come to a downhill 330-yard par 4, with a small lake 250 yards off the tee. But if the hole is playing downwind, he might easily be able to fly a drive over and beyond the lake, so he might approach the hole like a par 3 and try to knock his tee shot onto the green. However, if he played the same hole into a gale-force wind, the lake would be right where his tee shot could land, so he would probably approach the hole as a par 4 and hit an iron to lay up short of the lake off the tee.

ONE SHOT AT A TIME

When I was playing golf for a living, I never played as well as I could have played because I evaluated myself based on my score. If I was a few strokes under par in the middle of a round, I would suddenly feel uncomfortable because that was a lower score than I was used to shooting. That uncomfortable feeling impaired my abilities, so my scores immediately ballooned.

I had the ability to shoot low scores, but rarely did, because I never played the game one shot at a time. I was always trying to shoot a score, relating one shot to the next, instead of doing the best I could on every shot and not letting the past or the future influence the present. After starting a round poorly, I'd partially give up, and as a result of not trying too hard, I would often begin to play better. I developed a comfort zone around par. If I was on track to shoot below par, I'd get nervous and make some bogeys. If I was headed for a round higher than 72, I'd get mad, give up, relax, and consequently make some birdies.

My inability to stay focused on the present was a major factor in why I never succeeded as a tour professional. I hit the ball well enough to be successful, but I got distracted too easily and as a result my scores were too high.

During the 1977 Alberta Open, a Canadian tour event, I shot 75 in the first round. I hit the ball great, but took a million putts. In the second round, I shot 44 with 22 putts on the front nine, ending the nine with a four-putt for a double-bogey. I was disgusted and didn't care what happened on the back nine. That casual attitude freed up my abilities. I was no longer wound up in a knot over my score.

Guess what? I shot 32 on the back nine. I went back to my hotel, packed my bags, and flew home to Long Beach. To this day, I still don't know if my 75–76 – 151 made the cut. That round was the final straw. I finally understood that once you reach a certain skill level, your mindset, not your swing, determines how low you shoot. Technique is important, but it can only take you so far.

Many kids think like I should have thought at the beginning of my playing career. They don't seek a 'right' score. On the first tee, they don't think, 'It's windy today, and the greens are fast, so I should shoot around ninety.' Adults are more likely to put number limitations on themselves, and the limits ruin their golf games. If I tell a child that she can shoot in the 50s, she'll believe me. Why not? Some kids are that good, so I'm not going to tell them that they should shoot 72 when they could shoot 59.

When I talk golf with kids, I try to avoid asking how they played. If I ask, 'What did you shoot?' their feelings about their games will be predicated on how they scored. I try to get them to stop thinking about the score. So instead, I'll ask, 'Did you learn anything?' or 'What was the best shot you hit today?' If the child is one of my students, I might ask, 'Did you have a high percentage of shots in which you gave your best effort?' It's important that adults don't contaminate this childlike mindset.

Measuring yourself by your effort is perhaps the best way to judge yourself on the course. It's a technique I learned by reading about Orel Hershiser, the former Dodgers pitcher. He said that he pitched one pitch at a time, focusing on striving to throw the best pitch he could. Hershiser understood that he had no control over the hitter, so he concentrated on what he could control – the pitch he was about to throw.

The same is true in golf. All you can control is your effort. Your lie, the wind, how the ball reacts once it hits the ground, how other people play – all those things are beyond your control. Short-game teacher Dave Pelz has said that perfectly struck putts often don't go in the hole because of uneven green conditions. Once the ball leaves the clubface, it's no longer in your control. That's why you've got to do all you can to be in control of what happens *before* it leaves the clubface.

MY GOAL

My goal is to walk off the golf course feeling satisfied about my effort and how I played relative to my ability and the conditions. I never compare myself to how Tiger or Karrie Webb would have played. But many golfers do make such comparisons, and they don't understand the hurtful effects such comparisons have on their attitudes and, consequently, their games. We've all heard someone say something like, 'I made a six on the 14th hole, but my friend would have easily had a four.' The person who made a six is actually hurting his game, because he thinks he should have shot a score that is far superior to what he's capable of shooting. Thus, he's likely to leave the course feeling dejected, when he should be happy. The only comparison you should ever make in golf – if you make any comparison – is to the par system that's most appropriate to you and your skill level.

When playing golf, just do the best you can, and if you want to evaluate your game, use the personal par system that's appropriate to you.

12. IMAGINATION AND CREATIVITY
IF YOU CAN DREAM IT, YOU CAN DO IT

Who first thought walking on the moon was possible? Some lunatic, for sure. How about running a 4-minute mile? Climbing to the top of Mt Everest? Exploring the bottom of the oceans? More lunatics, every single one of the thinkers who believed those things were possible.

But they *were* possible.

Indeed, many of the most interesting and exciting things that humans have accomplished and invented were once said to be the stuff of dreams. But creative thinkers proved they were possible and made them into reality.

Before we go any further, I'd like you to do yourself a huge favour. Please erase the word 'impossible' from your mental dictionary. Why? Because the impossible is almost always possible. But to make the impossible happen, or to discover something original, you have to dream big, think carefully and then work super-hard to make the dreams come true. How huge should you dream? You can't dream too big, because there's always somebody else dreaming bigger.

How can you be exceptional if you can only do and think what average people do? You can't! To be great in golf, and in other activities, and to maximise your enjoyment in them, you have to think outside the box. You have to be an original thinker, utilising every ounce of your creativity and imagination.

Adults want to organise activities, including golf, into little mental boxes so that everything fits, nice and neat. They want well-defined ground rules, guidelines and plans so they know in advance how something is going to play out. Thinking like that is no good, though, because it breeds mediocrity. It fosters an attitude that makes you play within boundaries, sets unnecessary goals and limits your potential for achievement.

It's possible to hit an approach shot to 2 feet from the hole. Everybody agrees on that. But we don't all agree that it can be done 18 holes in a row. If you don't think it's possible to hit it stiff 18 consecutive times, you have no chance of doing it.

In everything you do – golf, writing, snowboarding, cooking – you're not going to maximise your success rate unless you have an open mind and are willing to challenge yourself always to do something different and, perhaps, better than you, or anybody else, has done before.

That's exactly what Tiger Woods does. Winning major championships by 15 strokes? Nine PGA Tour events in a single season? Piping low 255-yard 2-iron tee shots down the fairway? Playing an entire British Open at St Andrews without hitting into a single bunker? Tiger has done those things, but he has also dreamed of accomplishing more – much more. That's why he has redefined what tour players believe is possible. Virtually everybody on the PGA Tour – from young guns like Charles Howell to veterans like Hal Sutton – openly admits that Tiger has forced them to set their goals significantly higher than they were before he came along.

What's the best aspect of Tiger's attitude? That he can stay in the present, hitting one shot at a time. If he does that, he has the ability to win every tournament he enters – and he, better than anybody, knows that.

Playing great golf requires dreaming big, doing what seems to be impossible, creating shots that nobody has ever tried. Okay, time to start creating and dreaming!

CREATIVITY: A RECIPE FOR SUCCESS

Creativity is a big reason the Atascadero High School boys' golf team has for the last decade been one of the best squads in California, despite the school's relatively small student body. The Hounds, winners of the 2000 and 2001 California Interscholastic Federation Central Coast Regional Championship, spend much of their free time on the practice tee and the putting green at Chalk Mountain Golf Course. But they don't just beat balls. They use their practice time the way I'd like to see everybody practise. They're always playing games, having competitions, and trying to one-up each other, and I often participate in their antics. I love challenging the teenagers to contests such as, who can hit the longest 9-iron? or who can hit a drive that flies over 250 yards but never rises above the tree-line?

Justin Hendrix, who graduated in 2001, began his career on the junior varsity and played his last couple seasons with the varsity. For several years, Justin had wanted to hit his driver off the deck (i.e. the ground) but he couldn't do it. During his senior season, he saw me whacking my driver off the ground at the practice tee, and he admitted that he'd never been able to hit that shot. I gave him a few pointers – most important, take the same swing he would for a regular tee shot, but open the clubface a smidgen at address – and after a little experimenting Justin was hitting excellent shots with his driver off the ground. Best of all, Justin played a round the same day I showed him the shot, and he reached a par 5 in two shots for the first time because he hit his driver off the fairway on the approach.

WHEN SHOULD YOU BEGIN CREATING AND DREAMING?

From day one, the first time you ever touch a golf club. Don't get caught in the rut of practising every concept precisely as my book (or another book or instructor) suggests. Allow your imagination to run wild as soon as you begin learning to play golf. Experiment.

Being creative in golf isn't about learning totally new techniques. Rather, it involves taking the basics – your swing, address and grip – and making slight modifications to create new shots. In golf, small adjustments often produce huge differences. For example, you might be shocked by how much difference a little tweak to your grip can make in the flight pattern of a shot. Rotate your hands a little from left to right, and that might make the ball curve drastically from right to left, if you're a right-hander.

Learning to make small adjustments to standard positions gives you a much broader shot-making base. It prepares you to be comfortable in all conditions, and to be able to play without fear. If on a 160-yard approach to the green the wind is howling into your face so hard that you can't wear a hat, you – being a creative thinker – will know exactly how to hit a good shot close to the flag. You'll know to open the clubface a little at address, move the ball a little back in your stance, and swing a little more up and down. The result will be a low hummer that whistles below the wind, onto the green and stops near the hole.

WHAT DOES BEING CREATIVE REQUIRE?

It requires you first to master the basics, and then personalise them. Creativity in golf involves conjuring up ways to hit shots that you've never seen or may think are impossible.

Your ball is in the woods. You've got overhanging limbs, a small opening to the green, a lie on hardpan and a 120-yard shot? No problem. You might hit down on a 5-iron, taking a three-quarter swing, opening the clubface a little and trusting your instincts to hit with the right amount of power.

The only way to develop creativity is to practise a thousand different shots in your spare time, both at the range and on the course. Try to hit the ball exceptionally high with a driver and very low with a sand wedge. Feel the difference between a normal swing with a sand wedge that hits a standard shot and an exaggerated swing with the sand wedge that makes the ball go low. It's impossible to spend too much time cultivating your sense of imagination. You won't need to hit unusual shots all the time, but you'll use them a lot more often than you think. And the skills you learn when practising offbeat shots will make you a much better golfer, mentally and physically.

Creativity doesn't have a formula. Five golfers might each use a different method to hit a low 90-yard approach into a stiff breeze. One player might use a sand wedge and decide to hood, or shut, the clubface at address, while another golfer will choke down on the grip with a 9-iron. Creativity demands that you use what works best for you.

Creative shot-making has three steps:

1. Imagine the shot in your head.
2. Create a swing that will make the ball do what your imagination envisioned.
3. Hit the shot.

I hope you will, at least sometimes, imagine practice shots that are so outlandish that you won't be able to hit them. For example, think of a shot that for the first 50 yards flies low and hard, and then floats high and soft for the final 50 yards. Pushing your imagination to the limit is the only way to learn what you can do with all your different clubs. Try to hit high floaters with your 3-iron, and you'll learn just how high you can hit with that club. I bet it will be much higher than you had imagined.

ROGER AND ME

I had a memorable experience during a round with Roger Tambellini in March 2001. Roger grew up in Templeton, 20 miles north of San Luis Obispo, my home town, attended Atascadero High and was a student in my junior programme. After that, he was an All-America golfer at USC, and now he's a tour professional who, in 2001, played on mini-tours in Australia, Canada and the United States.

On a par 5 at Hunter Ranch Golf Course in Paso Robles, I pulled my second shot way left, and it landed on the tee of the adjoining hole. I was only 40 yards from the green, but it looked like I wouldn't be able to play my third shot at the green because I was blocked by a large row of trees. But I never say never until I've inspected every scenario. In this case, I saw a small opening to the green. The leaves on the trees didn't hang too low, and the grass had been trampled down between the green and me.

I imagined taking a short but powerful less-than-full swing motion to punch the ball hard and low, making it bound over the turf and onto the green. The only question was, what club do I need to hit a shot that won't travel too high off the ground? The answer: my putter. I wasn't surprised after I hit the shot exactly as I'd planned, and it stopped 6 feet from the hole.

Roger was shocked. 'Rudy, how'd you do that?' he said. 'Creativity,' I replied, smiling. 'Thinking big.'

THANKS, MR SNEAD, BUT I'LL DO IT MY WAY

If you can imagine a shot, you can feel it. And if you can feel a shot, you can hit it. As a child, Tiger proved those words to be true thousands of times. Two of the most memorable occurrences happened when he was six.

The first was during an exhibition that Tiger played with Sam Snead at Soboba Springs Royal Vista Golf Course in Hemet, California. The first hole we played with Sam was a 200-yard par 3 with a pond that was short and right of the green. Tiger hit a good tee shot with his driver, but he couldn't reach the green, and the ball rolled down the sloped fairway and into the edge of the pond.

To most people, Tiger's ball looked like it was in the water and thus unplayable. Tiger had a different perspective. He saw the ball as being only half submerged and playable. Tiger especially disliked taking penalty strokes, and he knew that lifting his ball out of the water would have required him to take a one-stroke penalty. So he decided to hit his approach from the half-submerged lie.

Snead had a puzzled look as he watched Tiger analysing his options. After all, it was only an exhibition, so why should Tiger have even considered attempting a miracle shot? Snead suggested that Tiger pick the ball out of the water and hit from the dry turf. But Tiger had already made up his mind.

Tiger addressed the ball, bobbed his head up and down to and from the target a few times, and then took a big swing. His club caused a big splash when it hit the water, but the ball sailed into the air, landed short of the green, took a few bounces and rolled into the middle of the green.

During a different exhibition, Tiger and I were playing a match against a team consisting of a club professional and a child. We were on the 12th hole at Chalk Mountain, a 194-yard downhill par 3 with a narrow creek crossing the fairway about 100 yards from the tee. A cartpath served as a bridge over the creek.

Because Tiger's best drive would fly 100 yards, the creek was in the middle of his intended landing area. His goal, though, was to get over the creek. I knew he wanted to get across the creek, but I didn't see how that was possible, so I thought he'd lay up. No chance.

Tiger created a shot that involved bouncing the ball over the cartpath. Tiger hit his driver, and the ball landed a few yards short of the path, bounced onto it, over it, and down the fairway, stopping 50 yards from the green. Tiger knocked his next shot onto the green, and he two-putted for a four.

Meanwhile, I was hacking around and made a five.

Can you imagine a golfer dominating the PGA Tour like Tiger has done? What about a golfer so good that he dominates Tiger?

Imagination has no limits. You can imagine golf shots in your bedroom before you go to sleep or on the bus going to school. You can practise them on the golf course, the driving range, the putting green, the chipping area, in your backyard or in your living room.

My favourite place is the putting green. I try to bounce the ball off the flagstick so the ball ricochets into a neighbouring hole. I try to hit 360 degree *lip outs*, in which the ball begins going in the hole, but does not, instead rolling all the way around the edge of the hole and then jumping back out onto the green. I try to hit the ball just hard enough so it hits the backside of the hole, bounces up into the air and falls down into the hole. I try to hit the ball so it dribbles over the front edge of the hole and into it.

Amazingly, you can practise all these shots from within three feet of a hole on the putting green. If you can do so much work in such a small space, imagine the variety of practising you can do throughout the entire grounds of a golf course? The work could last a lifetime.

Imagination and creativity is not a magic-formula method of learning and playing golf. Just the opposite, in fact. Hitting good golf shots is a result of big thinking, diligent practice and demonstration. Luck has nothing to do with good golf.

The following pages present a variety of situations that demand imagination, along with my recipe for creating shots appropriate to the circumstances. I've also provided drills and concepts to improve your creativity and stimulate your mind. This chapter should be a springboard, launching you into a never-ending quest to create, imagine, learn and achieve the *possible*.

PRACTISE WITH YOUR EYES CLOSED

PUTTING

Pick a hole on a practice green where you can hit straight, flat and uphill 6-foot putts. Place a ball on the green 6 feet from the hole, and address the ball. Take a few practice swings and rock your head back and forth between the ball and the hole as you take the practice swings. After the practice swings, line up your putter behind the ball. Now close your eyes. Make the same stroke you did during the practice swing, and hit the ball. Practise hitting putts with your eyes closed either for a predetermined time (10 minutes is good) or until you make five in a row from 6 feet. After mastering the 6-footer, begin using the eyes-closed method on putts of different lengths.

When you close your eyes while putting, your mind focuses exclusively on making the proper swing motion. Closing your eyes allows you to hone in on what's important – making a good swing – and to forget about everything else. Your mind will be free to feel the stroke.

This drill teaches you that distance is instinctive. Learning to hit the ball the correct distance is not a physical technique. It's a feel, or sense, that you develop through practice.

I putted for a couple of years with my eyes closed in the late 1980s, and I putted very well. Some tour professionals, including Mark Calcavecchia and Vijay Singh, have even putted with their eyes closed.

PLAYING

In his book *The Natural Golf Swing*, George Knudson says this about hitting a golf ball: 'The ball simply gets in the way of the motion.' I love that concept.

You don't need to focus on the ball at address, because if the ball is in the proper position and if you make a good swing, you will hit a good shot. You don't have to watch the club hit the ball. By being correctly set up and making a good swing, the club will properly hit the ball, propelling it on the path you had wanted it to travel. That's why you can close your eyes while hitting regular shots on the practice range and the course.

Hit a few shots with your eyes closed every time you go to the range, and play a couple of holes closing your eyes on each shot once in a while.

BUNKER BASICS

Bunker shots are among the most fun in the game, and they require precise and imaginative thinking. You can swing really hard in a bunker and the ball won't always go very far. Why? Because the sand wedge has a lot of loft, and several types of bunker shots – namely, those that need to get up quickly and land softly – require you to open the clubface at address to increase its loft.

The sand wedge has a flange on the back of the bottom side of the clubhead. The flange keeps the clubhead from digging into the sand, and instead makes the club bounce, or skid, through the sand. That's why you swing more up and down, or vertically, in bunkers than you do on normal full swing shots. The goal is to drive the club down into the sand so the clubhead slides under the ball and pops it up into the air.

When the flange hits the sand, it should be going fast enough to make a *thump*. You won't make that noise unless the flange first hits the sand, not the ball. If the leading edge of the clubhead hits the sand first, the clubhead will get stuck in the sand and you'll hit a bad shot. The *thump* is a key indicator that you have swung correctly.

I suggest you go into a bunker and practise. On every swing you should hear a solid *thump*. Use the full swing motion, picking the club up a little extra quickly in the backswing and then going straight down in the downswing. Your club should hit the sand two inches behind the ball.

Imagine that you're trying to drive the club down to the bottom of the bunker. Don't worry about swinging too steeply or digging your club into the sand. If you swing properly, the flange won't allow the club to get stuck in the sand.

Until I learned how the flange made the club glide through the sand, my bunker play was not very good. Now I look forward to being in bunkers because I know precisely what the ball will do if I make a good swing.

Many students fret about what size swing they should use in bunkers. Well, the swing size is different for everybody. A general rule, however, is that your swing should be fairly large – close to a full swing – on most sand shots. You vary the amount of loft, the pace of your swing and even the type of club to hit different distances and trajectories. You don't always use a sand wedge, even from around the green. A pitching wedge would be good from a greenside bunker on a shot that requires a lot of roll.

THERE ARE NO BAD LIES
Every lie is an opportunity to hit a great shot. It doesn't matter if your ball's fluffed up on a tuft of grass, against a tree root or buried in a bunker. In almost every circumstance, you *can* hit a good shot. You might not be successful, but the shot *is* possible.

The problem is that many golfers deviate from their normal routines when they have a so-called bad lie, and deviating throws off your swing and usually causes a bad shot. I hope, though, that you'll be smart enough to play with the attitude that 'no lie is a bad lie'. Embrace every situation you face on the golf course.

What other people may call a bad lie is just an opportunity to be creative. Concocting a variety of shots during a round is fun. To be prepared for all situations you might encounter during a round, it's necessary to become familiar with how the ball flies from different lies. To do that, you've got to practise from different lies. Drop balls into peculiar lies around the chipping green and the driving range, and hit shots with different clubs from each of the lies. Step on a ball so it's partially buried in the ground and hit a 3-wood. Put a little branch next to a ball and hit a wedge. Place balls in a divot and with a 9-iron hit six different trajectories, from very high to very low.

GETTING GYPPED

You can't get gypped in golf.

Getting gypped is a mindset. It's not an event. If you think your ball should always be teed up on a perfect tuft of grass, you don't understand golf, and you have no chance to play well or have fun. Even if you pipe a drive, your ball might land in a divot or a footprint in a bunker. Stuff happens. To play your best, you have to be unfazed by such situations.

Rather, approach every situation as an opportunity to hit a great shot. When your ball is plugged in a bunker, don't think about how easy a shot you would have had if your ball hadn't plugged. Assess how to hit the shot at hand; not the shot you believe you should have had.

HOW TO PLAY FROM UNUSUAL LIES

BURIED LIES IN A SAND BUNKER

It's tempting to think you have to scoop, or lift, the ball out of a buried lie in a bunker. But you don't.

Dig your feet into the sand and take a balanced stance, preparing for a powerful swing. Take your most lofted club and close the clubface a little at address. Position the ball a little back from the middle of your stance to encourage a descending blow. Take a steep, straight-up backswing, and then plough the club straight down on the angle of attack. Try to drive the leading edge of the clubhead into the sand, making first contact with the sand directly behind the ball. This is different from a regular bunker shot, in which you contact the turf two inches behind the ball.

The ball won't have any backspin when it hits the green, so it will roll much more than it would after a sand shot from a normal lie. Depending on how deep the ball is buried, you may not be able to get out of the bunker in one shot. That's OK. You can still get up-and-down in two by hitting one shot from the buried lie to a good lie, and then hitting the shot from the good lie into the hole.

DIVOTS
If your ball is in a divot hole, position the ball a little back in your stance from normal at address and try to hit the ball with a steeper downswing than you would use on a normal full swing. Don't do anything else differently. Stay in perfect balance and take your normal swing. There's plenty of loft on every club to hit a good shot out of most divots. Hit practice shots out of divots on the driving range with your low-irons and fairway woods. You'll be surprised at how well you can hit out of divots.

GETTING OUT OF THE WOODS
If you hit a shot into the trees, your imagination is your ticket out. Imagine a range of shots that will fly back to a good position, and select the shot that has the best balance between risk and reward. When in trouble, your first goal is to get back into play. Sometimes the most realistic recovery will be a shot to the green, but it might also be a 50-yard punch sideways and back to the fairway. Remember, you're in the woods – a bad place – and your goal is to get out of the woods and into a good place in the fewest possible strokes.

Your lie might not be great and your swing could be restricted, so you might need to invent a shot or a swing feel that you've never practised. Tour professionals do this all the time. You can tell they're creating a new shot when you see them taking an unusually large number of practice swings before hitting out of trouble. In such situations, the pro is giving himself a crash course in how to hit the shot. He is developing the address position, swing speed, grip and other techniques that are necessary for the shot.

As you practise inventing recovery shots and improve your ability to successfully hit them, you'll begin amazing not only yourself but also your playing partners. So the next time you hit a shot and somebody says, 'You're dead,' you can smile and reply not with words, but with a creative and successful shot.

THE FLOP SHOT

The flop is a really high shot that doesn't go very far and usually stops close to where it lands. You use the flop mostly around the green, and it's effective from all different lies.

With your most lofted club – probably a lob wedge – open the clubface at address. That means the back of the clubface should be closer to being parallel to the ground than it was before you adjusted it. Don't do anything special to your grip. While swinging, let your wrists bend softly but thoroughly in a way that adds extra loft to the club.

I think of the flop shot as a full swing that hits the ball almost nowhere. Most of the energy goes into snapping your wrists at impact to swipe the clubface under the ball, hitting it straight up. You'll see this shot a lot in the US Open because the rough around the greens is so thick that players can't play 'bump-and-runs'. They also need to flop the ball up so it'll land softly on the rock-hard greens.

Most people use the flop exclusively with their most lofted wedge, but you can use the flop technique with any club, even the driver. A great way to learn the flop is to stand close to a small tree and practise hitting over it. The closer you can stand and get over the tree, the better.

I taught Tiger the flop when he was five and he loved it. Most kids enjoy trying to hit a ball really high so it doesn't roll after landing. One afternoon Tiger and I were hitting flops together on the practice green at Heartwell Golf Park. After having almost emptied our shag bags, I went to the green to retrieve the balls. To my surprise, Tiger continued hitting while I was picking up the balls. He hit one ball slightly off line, and it landed right on top of my head. Good thing Tiger was a quick learner, and knew how to hit the ball high and make it land softly.

DECONSTRUCTING GOLF

I learned one of the biggest lessons of my career by playing in a three-club tournament at Chalk Mountain Golf Course in the early 1980s. I used a 5-iron, a 9-iron and a putter. On the front nine I shot 46, but I played much better on the back and fired a 37, hitting eight of nine greens in regulation. It took me ten more nine-hole rounds, using my full set, to shoot lower than 37.

What happened during that magical nine of 37? I had broken golf down to its most basic element – a single swing that I trusted so much I could use it everywhere. I wasn't trying to create a new swing for every different shot. For a 140-yard approach, I'd take a little speed off the swing and hit a high floater. On tee shots, I let it fly. I hit little cuts and draws, just feeling my way to the target. I wasn't thinking of a specific technique; I just imagined each shot and let my feel take over.

Having a limited selection of clubs also put an additional element of fun into the competition. It was a new challenge, going to a course and not being stuck in my old habits.

SINGING IN THE RAIN

Playing in the rain can be just as much fun as playing in beautiful sunshine. The same is true for playing in cold, snow, wind or any other adverse condition. To play well, you need imagination to adjust your swing to accommodate for things such as extra clothes, damp lies, wet grips and the shorter distance the ball goes because of heavy air. Rain forces you to concoct a slightly different stance and grip to maintain good balance.

The key: think creatively. Never let weather be an excuse for bad golf. If it's raining on you, it's also raining on your playing partners and competitors, so everybody's battling the same thing.

Rain is an extreme playing condition, but no two days on a course are exactly the same. You won't maximise your ability as a golfer until you learn to adapt to golf's ever-changing situations. That's why tour professionals play practice rounds prior to a competition. During the rounds, they are not overly concerned with practising their swings. They want to become familiar with the course layout and adjust to the local conditions.

RAIN IS NO EXCUSE

I have a friend who played on his college golf team in upstate New York, and he played most of his tournaments in cold and damp weather. When he and his teammates didn't play well, they often blamed their poor performances on the weather. Doing that provided a modicum of comfort, but, in retrospect, my friend believes making excuses prevented him and his team from achieving their potential.

'If we would have admitted that we had let the weather affect our attitudes, and thus our game, we would have realised the true reason for our high scores,' my friend says. 'I wish we would have just played golf and forgotten about the weather.'

That's an invaluable lesson. As long as the weather, or any other external condition, affects your attitude, you won't play your best.

LESS IS MORE

I am a natural right-hander. But I switched sides and started playing golf left-handed in the late 1970s.

Lots of swing knowledge doesn't necessarily produce great results. Good golf is not, as I had thought, the result of knowledge alone. It comes from having the feel of solid hitting. It's largely dependent on the sixth sense you develop by playing games, hitting crazy shots and spending countless hours around the course letting the game soak into your system.

When Tiger was a little kid, he didn't have book-learned technical knowledge, which he does now. He hadn't studied the swing. However, the basics he learned from his dad, and from the rudimentary technique I gave him, provided enough understanding to hit the golf ball perfectly. He was like a baby eagle that could fly a few days after having broken out of the egg.

I never got too good as a left-handed golfer. I understood the technique I needed to hit good shots as a lefty, but I rarely hit them. Why? My lack of practice and feel. Playing left-handed taught me that you can't take knowledge to the course and instantly play well. If you could, I would have been immediately shooting in the 70s.

Playing from the left side made me stop trying to cram a bunch of knowledge into my students. Instead, I provide the minimum I think that they need to hit good shots, and I give them plenty of time and space in which to practise and develop their touch and feel.

13. Q & A
MY ANSWERS TO YOUR QUESTIONS

How do you learn something if you don't know anything about it? Ask an expert.

No question is a bad question. Teaching is a two-way street, and I enjoy having students and parents ask questions, because the best teaching environment is one in which everybody is constantly exchanging information. I learn a lot when I get asked questions; the queries show me how much the students know about the game and what I need to share with them. What's more, people often ask questions that I can't answer, so I'm forced to do research and learn new things.

Here are the questions I'm most frequently asked, along with my answers.

1. WILL MY CHILD BE AS GOOD AS TIGER?
Rarely do kids seriously compare themselves to Tiger, but some parents want to know if their child is a prodigy. Parents don't often ask this question directly, but rather in a roundabout way. They'll say, 'I know my child probably won't be as good as Tiger, but how good can he become?'

The answer depends on the student and his or her desire. I've seen plenty of students who might be talented enough to play professional golf one day, and I am sure that I will see many more. But whatever *I* say ultimately means very little. If pro golf is in the child's heart, he or she might – *might* – become a successful tour professional.

Tiger never tried to be as good as somebody else. His sole goal was to be as good a golfer as *he* could be. While Tiger admired some of golf's greatest players, I don't recall him ever comparing himself to another player. Tiger kept a list of Jack Nicklaus's tournament victories on his bedroom wall, but he used that list – and other players' records – only as motivational tools.

When I'm working with a talented student, passers-by will often say, 'Oh, is that the next Tiger Woods you're grooming?' My response is always the same: 'No, this is the current [student's name].'

WHY WATCH, WHEN YOU CAN PLAY?

I took Tiger to the Los Angeles Open, a PGA Tour event at Riviera Country Club, three times when he was a child, and I was always surprised by his total lack of interest. He always wanted to be somewhere else.

One year I brought Tiger to the range so we could watch the pros practise, because most people enjoy watching the pros up close. Tiger, however, was bored. Unlike most kids at the tournament, Tiger didn't try to get any autographs. He looked at me with a plain expression and said, 'Rudy, when can we leave and go play golf?'

2. DOES A BEGINNER NEED EXPENSIVE CLUBS?

Definitely not. No child or beginner needs expensive clubs to learn basic golf skills and develop his or her game. When Tiger first came to me, he had used cut-down clubs.

There are many high-quality, inexpensive golf clubs available. The rule with golf equipment is that there is not necessarily any correlation between the amount you spend on clubs and the quality of your game. The most important thing to consider when purchasing clubs isn't cost, but rather that they fit properly.

3. HOW OFTEN SHOULD A CHILD TAKE LESSONS? WHAT TYPE OF LESSONS SHOULD HE OR SHE TAKE?

One hour per month of one-on-one time with a PGA golf professional, coupled with regular group activity in a junior golf programme, is the ideal amount of activity for most kids. The same schedule is applicable to beginners of any age. But don't worry if you can't afford, or find, quality one-on-one teaching. What's most important is to enrol your child in a junior golf programme that has regular – preferably weekly – sessions and a summer schedule of tournaments.

Individual instruction probably won't be the most valuable part of your child's development as a golfer. Participating in a group programme is often much more helpful, especially in the beginning, because children learn the social aspects of the game along with swing technique.

4. IS ONE HOUR PER MONTH OF INDIVIDUAL ATTENTION ENOUGH IF A CHILD IS SUPER-TALENTED?

Absolutely. One hour a month is plenty of individual attention for a golfer at any skill level. A one-hour session with a good teacher will provide most golfers with more than enough concepts to tackle in a month. Lots of LPGA and PGA Tour players don't get monthly instruction. In his prime, Jack Nicklaus used to visit his teacher, Jack Grout, only at the beginning of every season.

It takes time to master a technique. Adults tend to think that they've learned a new concept after they've hit three good shots. If only golf were so simple. Kids, however, usually understand that you haven't mastered something until you've hit 1,000 good shots.

The exception to my one-hour rule is a child who really enjoys taking lessons and has a good relationship with the instructor. But the child – not the parent – should ask for the additional lessons.

5. HOW DO YOU SELECT A GOLF TEACHER?

Here are three qualifications to look for in a teacher for a child.

(a) A good player with tournament experience.
(b) Someone who has worked with an established junior programme for more than a year.
(c) A teacher who can provide access to a course.

The last item is perhaps the most important thing to look for in a prospective instructor. Indeed, access is the biggest barrier between kids and golf. Some families can't afford country club dues, while other families who live near good public facilities are left out in the cold because the courses don't allow juniors. Tiger's father, Earl, played at the Los Alamitos Navy Course in Long Beach, but that course had a minimum age of ten. Before Tiger reached that age, the course permitted him to play occasionally on its third nine, but he wasn't allowed on the regular course until he turned ten.

I had a firm policy at Heartwell Golf Park, allowing people of any age to be on the course if they could keep up with the group ahead and play by the rules. Tiger easily met both requirements at age four.

You should put the same care into finding a golf coach for your child as you would into selecting a school. Start by asking friends for recommendations. If nothing turns up, call the PGA section office that oversees courses in your neighbourhood. All PGA section offices have at least one person familiar with junior golf.

Once you have a list of pros, call each pro and make appointments to meet and interview them. During the initial phone conversation, tell the pro you want to get your child involved in golf and that you would like to interview them. Most pros, even those at private clubs where you might not be a member, will be receptive to your inquiries.

Here are some tips for contacting club professionals.

(a) Don't ask to meet on Saturday morning at 9:00 a.m. That's the busiest time for pros. And not on Mondays, either, because Monday is usually the pro's only day off. Tuesday and Thursday afternoons are generally the slowest days at both public and private courses.

(b) Set up an appointment in advance, and be clear that you're not scheduling a lesson.

(c) The pro shouldn't charge a fee for the consultation.

(d) Don't rule out lessons or programmes at private clubs if you're not a member. Lots of clubs have junior programmes that are open to the public. What's more, a pro who likes a child will often make room for the child in his programme even if the child isn't a member at the club.

(e) Visit the course when your child will be using it, most likely after school and on weekends. You want to gauge the course's atmosphere at those times.

Also consider the type of course. Is it junior-friendly? If it is, it won't have too much water or a lot of forced carries. Par 3 layouts, courses with forward tees on every hole and executive courses are ideal for juniors and beginners.

A child doesn't have to be groomed at a posh country club to become a good golfer. All of Tiger's early development happened at public courses, notably Heartwell Golf Park and Bellflower Golf Course, both in Southern California.

More important than whether a club is private or public is the friendliness of the entire staff, not just the pro. Does the course have a friendly and safe environment? Do you see other kids hanging around? How do the snack bar and pro shop employees treat children? It's definitely good to ask patrons at the course about the staff. You can also do your own reconnaissance. Send your child into the snack bar and the pro shop to see how he or she is greeted.

Definitely ask lots of questions when you meet the prospective pro. If he is a good teacher, he'll be happy to answer your queries. Here are some questions to ask.

(a) Does the course have a junior programme?
(b) Do juniors get discounted rates on greens fees? Practice balls? Equipment?
(c) Are there times when kids are barred from playing or practising?
(d) Is there a charge for practising, other than the fee for range balls? (There should be no extra charges.)
(e) Can patrons bring their own lunch? Will there be a problem if the child brings his own lunch to the snack bar? (You shouldn't have to buy something at the snack stand in order to eat there.)

(f) Does the junior programme include tournaments? Are there additional junior tournaments in your area? Competition will be a vital part of a child's golf development, no matter what her or his goals are. Most kids enjoy fun competitions, and it gives them a chance to demonstrate what they're learning. I've always had weekly stroke-play tournaments in my junior programme.

(g) Does the pro, or a member of his or her staff, cut down clubs for kids? Not all courses do this, but if the course where your child plays doesn't offer this service, you must find a reliable place to get clubs properly fitted for your children.

WHY DID THE WOODSES BRING TIGER TO ME?

Tiger had unbelievable talent by the age of four. His parents recognised their son's precocious ability, and that's why they came to me. They had taught him everything they could about the game, so the next logical step was to find a teaching pro.

Why me? A few other teachers recommended me to the Woodses. I had a successful junior programme, I had a good amount of tournament experience and I had given lessons to some good players in Southern California, including Sue Bennett, who played on the LPGA, and Steve Cook, who had been runner-up at the 1969 US Public Links championship.

6. HOW INVOLVED SHOULD A PARENT BE IN HIS OR HER CHILD'S GOLF?

Just as involved as you are with your child's piano lessons or another sport in which they are involved. No more, no less. I prefer to have a modest amount of parental involvement.

Having a parent by the lesson tee helps me communicate with younger students. No matter how astute a child is, he won't remember everything a teacher tells him. That's where parents can help. When a parent watches a lesson, he or she also hears what the teacher says, and that enables the parent to continue to communicate proper golf information to the student when the teacher isn't around.

Here are some questions to ask yourself to gauge the proper level of involvement that you and your child should have in golf.

- Does your child want you to be involved in golf?
- Do you feel you *need* to be involved?
- Do you want to be involved?
- Will your involvement benefit both you and your child?
- Does your involvement help make your child more, or less, comfortable?

Do you need to be involved for your child to be successful? No. But involvement can take the form of non-golf support. Some of my most helpful parents don't play golf. Their support involves providing transportation and encouragement.

EARL AND TIDA'S INVOLVEMENT IN TIGER'S GOLF

Tiger's parents were very involved in their child's golf. Tiger's father, Earl, often accompanied Tiger to lessons, during which I'd teach both of them at the same time. Because Earl wasn't nearly as good a golfer as Tiger, I actually spent most of my time helping Earl, while Tiger would practise next to us.

Tiger's mother, Tida, took up golf when Tiger was five so she could play with him. Even though Tiger could handle the golf course alone at that age, he was too young to be left alone, and Earl and I couldn't always play with him.

Earl, Tiger and I regularly played together, and after the round we often had lengthy golf-talk sessions at the Woodses' home. The talks were wide-ranging, and we talked about many subjects besides golf. Earl and I did most of the talking, and Tiger did a lot of listening, providing some input. Earl often took notes. We watched lots of sports on TV and dissected our golf games and the game itself. What I most remember about these talks was that we never treated Tiger like a kid. He was just one of the guys.

7. ARE YOU TOO INVOLVED WITH YOUR CHILD'S GOLF?

Occasionally a child will tell me, 'My parents are making me learn to play golf.' Forcing a child to play golf rarely has a good result. Certainly, the child will show up for lessons if he or she is forced, but nobody – not the child, the parent or the teacher – has fun. Children have to want to play golf if they are going to improve. They have to want to take a lesson or attend a junior programme if they are going to get anything positive out of the experiences.

8. DO CHILDREN NEED TO PLAY TOP-NOTCH COURSES TO BECOME GREAT GOLFERS?

No. Anybody can adequately learn to play golf at any course. The quality of the course doesn't necessarily have anything to do with the quality of the instruction, or the ability the student will have to fulfil her or his potential. Some great teachers work at poorly maintained courses, and some inexperienced instructors work at premier clubs.

My junior programme has always been conducted on daily-fee public courses, none of which ever has hosted, or ever will host, a major championship. Nevertheless, dozens of alumni from the programme have had successful golf careers. Aside from Tiger, my programme's alumni include tour pros, club professionals, collegiate Division I and II scholarship recipients and state junior champions.

Most people think the average golf course is a private place with a big gate. That's not true. There are 16,700 courses in the United States, and 71 per cent of them are open to the public. On British public courses, the average weekend greens fee, for adults, is £20. Many of the public courses have deeply discounted rates for juniors and seniors. Virtually all public courses welcome juniors, although some have restricted times for the discounted rates. The Yellow Pages and the Internet are reliable sources to find public courses in your community.

9. HOW OFTEN SHOULD YOUR CHILD PRACTISE?

The more a golfer practises, the better he'll play. It's a simple equation without exceptions. But not wanting to practise isn't a bad thing. Golf doesn't have to be everybody's first priority. Some golfers want to play the game from dawn to dusk, and then some. Others are content playing once a month, while I know several people who tee it up twice a year and love every moment of their rounds.

No level of involvement is bad, and no level is better than another. As long as the golfer is making her or his own choice, it's a good choice.

That said, there's no magic formula for sparking somebody's interest in the game. But once somebody gets the golf bug, and they enjoy golf and want to practise, they'll improve quickly. When they don't enjoy the game and don't want to practise, it's time to store the clubs and find another activity.

When I was a kid, I couldn't wait to get home from school so I could play football in the street. If a child has a similar burning desire to go to the golf course, take him.

PATIENCE HAS ITS REWARDS

A good friend of mine is a lifelong golfer and devoted student of the game. He began dating a woman in college, and they married when they were in their late twenties. The woman had never played golf when she met my friend, and she never showed any interest in the game throughout the first ten years of their relationship.

My friend never prodded his wife to play. He thought that if he pushed her into the game, she'd probably rebel and shun the game forever. But when they reached their early thirties, the woman announced, out of the blue, that she wanted to play golf.

She took a lesson, which went well. She took another lesson, which went even better. She was an addict in no time, dragging her husband to the course and forcing him to watch golf on TV.

I can't guarantee that everybody will get hooked on golf like my friend's wife did. But if you are patient, you may be pleasantly surprised by the results.

10. HOW MUCH TIME CAN A CHILD BE AWAY FROM THE GAME BEFORE HER OR HIS GAME DETERIORATES?

It takes years for a child's game to go down the tubes. Taking the summer off to work or go to camp won't hurt a child's golf game. A break from the game might even be helpful, providing a chance to get away from it and develop an appreciation for it. Bill Cleary, who recently retired as the athletic director at Harvard University, has said he thinks it's terrible that so many kids focus all their efforts on one sport instead of playing lots of sports.

Golf is great, but so are other sports, and a child should play as many sports as he or she wants. I've had several students leave my programme for a few years and return to it swinging better than ever.

A break might even reinvigorate a golfer's passion. People often miss what they don't have.

11. SHOULD A CHILD PLAY IN TOURNAMENTS?

Yes. Competition is definitely good for children. I recommend starting your child in tournaments once he or she knows the rules of golf and can hit the ball into the hole on every green. Don't worry how many strokes it takes to get the ball into the hole; if they can hole out, that's good enough. Even children who have no desire to become top-ranked players enjoy the camaraderie and spirit of competition at junior events.

12. HOW FAST SHOULD A CHILD IMPROVE IN GOLF?

There's no set time for how long it'll take for anybody to achieve a certain level of competency. Tiger was tour-pro material when he was five, but some other tour pros, like Larry Nelson, didn't take up the game until they were nearly twenty years old.

The most important thing is to not set limits for a child. Always keep the door open. Every child learns the game at his own pace. If a child is interested in golf, he'll learn quickly because he'll seek out the necessary knowledge and dedicate the requisite practice time.

One of the benefits we have in golf is that it's not a required subject. It's a sport we play for fun and with friends.

A warning: If you are the parent of a son or daughter who likes golf, but doesn't seem to have much aptitude for the game, don't be concerned. It's not time to yank him off the course and sign him up for trumpet lessons. If the child is happy, he or she should continue playing golf. Some golfers who enjoy the game the most shoot the highest scores.

13. WHAT DO YOU HAVE TO SHOOT TO WIN LPGA AND PGA TOUR EVENTS?

You have to shoot *very* low. You have to average 65 on your home course when it's playing at its most difficult. That means you have to play from the tee markers that are so far back they're not even on the tees; every flagstick is in the most difficult position; the superintendent is on vacation and nobody mows the rough so it grows thicker than it does at the British Open; and the sprinklers on the greens must be permanently broken, so the greens get brick hard. Under those conditions, if you can shoot 65 every day, you might be able to win a tour event.

I'm exaggerating only slightly because the numbers are daunting. There are 60 million golfers on the planet, with more and more taking up the game daily. There are only 400 full-time players between the LPGA and PGA tours, so one of every 150,000 golfers is on one of the two major pro circuits.

Indeed, every year a total of about 60 new players qualify for the LPGA and PGA tours, combined. To make it, you've got to want to be on tour so badly that you are willing to make enormous sacrifices.

I often hear parents boast about their children's golf accomplishments. I know the parents hope I'll respond with something to this effect: 'Your child is doing great, and if she keeps it up the tour is a good possibility.' Rarely, though, do I utter such words.

Personal par is the best gauge to determine a child's stature on a national level. If a child averages 5 or more shots under her or his personal par, she or he is among the top players in the nation. Lots of kids shoot low rounds once in a while, but very few consistently do so.

14. DO YOU HAVE TO BE AS GOOD AS TIGER WAS AS A TEENAGER TO RECEIVE A COLLEGE GOLF SCHOLARSHIP?

It's *much* easier to get a golf scholarship than it is to be a successful tour pro. Scholarships are available to boys and girls who are exceptional golfers, but they don't have to be as good as Tiger was. Even if the student is a terrible golfer and an active caddie, several organisations offer caddie scholarships. The Evans Scholar Foundation, part of the Western Golf Association, gives scholarships and even has dormitories on some Midwestern college campuses for its scholarship recipients. Some companies that make golf course maintenance equipment have scholarship funds. A student from Penn State University who was training to become a golf course superintendent raised funds for a six-month internship with the grounds crew at the Old Course at St Andrews, in Scotland, by soliciting money from a collection of companies that manufacture golf course maintenance equipment.

You don't have to average 65 to get a college golf scholarship. Keep your grades and hopes up and your eyes open, and begin investigating the possibilities when you enter high school.

15. DO CHILDREN NEED GOLF SHOES?

No. From a playing perspective, nobody needs golf shoes unless he or she is playing in the rain or on a very wet course, where sliding around could be a problem and spikes will help the player to keep from slipping. You may want golf shoes, though, and there's nothing wrong with that. Just don't expect your score to go down because you wear golf shoes. You could even play barefoot. Sam Snead used to play without shoes when he was a young man practising in West Virginia.

The *Rules of Golf* don't require anybody to wear golf shoes on the course. Gabriel Hjertstedt, a PGA Tour player, used to wear sneakers in tournaments, and several Senior tour players wear golf sandals in competition. I play golf in spikeless teaching shoes.

Children should wear comfortable athletic shoes that have a little bit of tread to handle hilly terrain and wet grass. If your child wants to play in wet weather, you might consider getting waterproof golf shoes.

Whether you wear golf shoes is a question of fashion more than performance.

16. CAN CHILDREN WITH DISABILITIES PLAY GOLF?

Absolutely! There are blind golfers; golfers with no legs; golfers with no arms (they hold the club under their necks); and partially paralysed golfers, to name a few. Many of these people play golf quite well, too, and often compete in tournaments. Sometimes they compete against other golfers with disabilities, but they also compete against able-bodied players.

There's a man in my home town who has one leg and sometimes breaks 90. Dennis Walters is a famous trick-shot artist who performs out of a wheelchair because he's paralysed from the waist down. The Edwin Shaw Hospital for Rehabilitation in Akron, Ohio, has a golf course designed specifically for people with disabilities. The course has handrails on the tees, gentle inclines on the holes and wheelchair accessible paths.

You'll find plenty of information about golf for individuals with disabilities on the Internet.

17. ARE THERE GOLF CAMPS FOR KIDS?

There are lots of good golf camps for kids. A good place to find information about junior golf camps is to look at the advertisements in the back of golf magazines and on websites. There's a list of camps at www.juniorgolf.com. Also, many of the traditional golf schools for adults offer junior golf curricula.

18. ARE THERE CAREER OPTIONS IN GOLF BESIDES PLAYING AND TEACHING?

Yes, a million. Here are some golf course jobs that you might not know about.

● *Environmental consultant:* ensures courses are built to be environmentally friendly and meet governmental codes.

- *Computer manager and consultant:* among other duties pro-grammes the computer that manages the irrigation system.
- *Machinery salesperson:* sells the big mowers that are used to cut the fairways, greens and rough at golf courses.
- *Food and beverage manager:* decides what people eat at golf courses by managing a course's dining facilities.
- *Superintendent:* oversees the maintenance of a golf course, keeping the grass green, the trees tall, the bunkers smooth and full of sand, the ponds clean and the flowers beautiful.
- *Sports journalist:* does research at tournaments, courses, golfers' homes and golf conventions and writes articles and does TV and radio commentary. There are dozens of magazines about golf; many newspapers have weekly golf sections; and there's even a TV station devoted exclusively to golf – the Golf Channel.
- *Golf course designer:* creates the plan for the golf course.
- *Golf course builder:* drives bulldozers and uses shovels and other tools to move dirt and shape holes during the construction of a golf course. The builder executes the plan drawn up by the architect/designer.

19. WHAT SUMMER JOBS IN GOLF ARE AVAILABLE FOR KIDS?

Golf is a great industry for summer employment for youths. Schoolchildren can caddie, drive the tractor that picks up balls on the driving range, clean and maintain golf carts and work in the pro shop. Check with your local course to see what's available, but be sure to visit the course and talk to the head pro a few months before you want to start working. I tend to hire kids who play at the course, have a positive attitude and are friendly towards other golfers. Golf skill is not a require-ment. Desire to work hard is.

20. HOW CAN ONE TELL IF A CHILD IS BURNED OUT?

A child is burned out if you have to drag him to the course or if he isn't having fun playing golf. Do kids ever get burned out from throwing a baseball with friends? No. If you let a child decide how often he or she wants to play golf, he or she will rarely get burned out. Do your best to make golf fun for you and your child, and you'll probably never have to worry about burnout.

When I taught Tiger, people often asked me if he ever became burned out because he practised so often and played up to twenty junior tournaments a year. I always answered the burnout question by saying, 'Tiger is having so much fun, I can't imagine why he'd get burned out.'

The truth is, Tiger wanted to play golf as much as possible. It was his parents who had to rein in his enthusiasm.

21. CAN GIRLS PLAY FROM THE BOYS' TEES?

Yes. All golfers should vary the tees from which they play. Alternating tees from round to round gives you the opportunity to play different shots on the same hole. For example, a 170-yard par 3 will always be a 170-yard par 3 if you constantly play the same tee. But if you alternate tees from round to round, you'll find the hole probably varies from 140 to 170 yards, and the variety will make the game more fun and interesting.

Long hitters can benefit by playing from forward tees because they'll make more birdies, and that'll build their confidence. Short hitters can benefit by playing from back tees because they'll have the chance to practise their long clubs that they might not normally use.

With enough practice, girls can beat boys from the same tees. Vicki Goetze, now an LPGA player, played from the boys' tees throughout her childhood, and she won a Georgia high school boys' championship. Remember, in golf everything is possible.

22. ARE THERE AGE REQUIREMENTS FOR DRIVING GOLF CARTS?

There's no national age requirement for driving a golf cart. Each course sets its own regulation. At the two courses that I own, the minimum age for driving a cart is 18.

23. WHO IS THE IDEAL GOLF PARTNER?

No matter your skill level, I suggest that you play with the most highly skilled and friendliest golfers you can find. If you don't know the best, most patient and friendliest players at your course, get to know them. Age is irrelevant. It's the quality of the players that matters. It's perfectly appropriate for an 11-year-old to play with a 48-year-old. My father, a 14-handicapper who's in his seventies, often enjoys playing with juniors. Don't rule out the possibility of playing with the golf pro at your course. Just ask her or him, and you'll be surprised how often the pro will make time to play with you.

If your goal is to be the best player you can, then you need to play golf with the best players available. On the professional tours, the best players tend to practise together, and lesser players, especially rookies, practise together.

When I played tournament golf, I never thought of myself as one of the best players. I felt that I was an average touring pro who was learning to be a good one, which was true. But by limiting my playing circles to golfers at my skill level, I robbed myself of the opportunity to assimilate the qualities and mindset of the most skilled players.

One thing I would definitely do differently given the chance to relive my days as a tour pro is to go on to the driving range at every tournament, find the best player I could, regardless if he was a friend, and ask him to play a practice round with me. If he said no, I'd go to the second-best player, and down the line, until somebody said yes.

BLUE-COLLAR CHAMPIONS

Every year there's a Ryder Cup-format competition for men pitting teams from Chalk Mountain Golf Course, a public facility that I own, and San Luis Obispo Country Club, a private course at which I'm a member. It's fun to watch the tournament because of my close ties to each course. You might think the country club team, whose members play a more difficult and better-conditioned course than the Chalk players, would routinely beat Chalk Mountain. However, the opposite has happened. By the end of 2000, Chalk Mountain had won six of the eight matches since the event was first held in 1993. The country club golfers are too used to playing among a relatively small circle of friends and at the same course all the time. The public course players travel more to new courses, and they are used to competing in different conditions, which gives them more well-rounded games.

14. DICTIONARY
GOLF HAS ITS OWN LANGUAGE

Golf uses everyday words in ways that often have little to do with their common usage. A chopper isn't a helicopter; it's a bad golfer. A rock isn't something you climb; it's a golf ball. There's nothing in this dictionary that will make you hit the ball better. But by learning these words and terms, you'll be able to better communicate with your fellow golfers and feel more comfortable around the course.

This dictionary isn't a complete list of every golf word and phrase. It simply includes my favourites.

Ace: a hole-in-one.

Address: the position you take over the ball just prior to beginning the swing.

Albatross: a score of 2 on a par 5.

Approach shot: a full-swing shot to a green.

Apron: a rarely used term for the fringe, or first cut of grass surrounding the green.

Away: the person whose ball is farthest from the hole is 'away'.

Backspin: backward spinning of the ball.

Bag toter: a caddie.

Bail-out area: the safe side of a green, fairway or other part of a hole.

Ball-in-pocket: description of a person who has finished playing a hole or a round.

Ball marker: a coin, or other item, used to mark your ball on the putting surface.

Ballmark: a dent made in the green by the ball.

Banana: a shot that curves too much from left to right, for a right-handed player.

Bats: golf clubs.

Beach: a sand *bunker* (often called a 'sand trap').

Birdie: a score of 1 under par on a hole.

Blade: a style of iron clubhead that is primarily flatbacked and usually forged.

Bladed: what you've done when you've hit a shot with an iron that flies super fast and super low. It happens when the leading edge of the club hits the middle of the ball.

Blind shot: a shot to a target that can't be seen.

Blue dart: a snap-hook.

Bogey: a score of 1 over par on a hole.

Bump 'n' run: a shot, usually to a green, that rolls a long way after hitting the ground.

Bunker: a big hole on the course, usually with sand in it.

Bunter: a short hitter; to *bunt* is to hit a short shot.

Cabbage: tall, thick grass.

Carry: the distance the ball travels in the air from where it's hit to where it lands.

Cart barn: where golf carts are stored.

Chilli-dip: a shot in which the club hits the turf well behind the ball, causing it to dribble forwards; usually happens on shots around the green.

Choke: play badly, usually under pressure.

Chopper: a bad golfer.

Chunk: same as chilli-dip, except you dig up a little more turf and the club makes even less contact with the ball.

Collar: another word for fringe.

Committee: the group of people who are in charge of the rules at a golf tournament.

Course rating: one of two gauges for measuring the difficulty of a course. The rating is based primarily on distance. Course rating and slope are used together to determine a course's overall difficulty.

Cow pasture: a poorly maintained course.

Cow-pasture pool: the game of golf.

Cross-bunker: a bunker that lies across the middle, or a significant portion, of a fairway.

Crowned green: a green whose high point is in the middle; shaped like an army helmet.

Cup: an incorrect but commonly used word for the hole in the green.

Dance floor: the putting green.

Dawn patrol: first group of golfers out on the course in the morning.

Dead: no chance to hit a good shot ('You're dead'); also, a term for a shot that's very close to the hole ('That shot is dead').

Dewsweeper: somebody who plays early in the morning.

Dimples: the small depressions on a golf ball.

Divot: a chunk of turf dug out of the ground by your club.

Dogleg: a hole that curves to the right or to the left.

Double-eagle: another word for Albatross.

DQ'd: disqualified from a competition.

Draino: a description of a putt that goes in the hole.

Draw: a shot that curves slightly from right to left, for a right-handed player.

Drink: a water hazard.

Drowned it: hit into the water.

Duck: a bad player.

Duck hook: a shot that curves severely from right to left, for a right-handed player.

Duck soup: a group of bad golfers.

Eagle: a score of 2 under par on a hole.

Etiquette: behaviour on the golf course.

Fade: a shot that curves slightly from left to right, for a right-handed player.

Fan: the wind. 'The hole is into the fan.'

Fan it: to swing and miss the ball.

Fat: a shot in which your club hits the turf before it hits the ball, and the ball doesn't go very far.

Fill it up: make a good putt.

First cut: the shortest cut of rough.

Flagstick: the stick that holds the flag and rests in the hole.

Flatback: another word for a blade.

Flatstick: a putter.

Flop shot: a shot deliberately hit as high as possible with a lofted club from around the green; the ball usually lands gently and rolls very little after landing.

Flub: a shot in which your club hits the turf way behind the ball, even farther behind than on a fat shot.

Foot wedge: moving the ball with your foot from a bad lie to a good lie.

Fore: what you yell to warn people when your ball is, or could be, headed in their direction.

Forged iron: a type of iron clubhead that is hammered and ground into shape.

Fried egg: a ball that's partially buried below the surface in a sand bunker.

Fringe: the cut of grass surrounding a green.

Gag: another term for choke.

Getting the job done: shooting a good score, on a hole or for a round, despite not hitting a lot of good shots.

Gimme: a putt your partners don't require you to hole out but which counts as if it were holed; according to the official rules, gimmes are illegal in stroke play, but they are permitted in match play.

Goat track: another term for cow pasture.

Going ballistic: getting mad.

Grinder: a golfer who practises a lot; a golfer who tries incredibly hard on every shot while playing.

Grooved: a description of a golfer who's swinging well and feels like every shot's going to be great.

Grooves: the long, narrow cuts in the surface of the clubface. Both irons and woods have grooves.

Gross: your raw score.

Gunch: a bad place for your ball to be ('It's in the gunch').

Gut-check: a short putt that you should make but could miss, usually at a critical point in a round or match.

GV (pronounced 'Gee-five'): a Gulfstream V personal jet, which you can afford when you shoot low enough often enough. Approximate cost: $40 million. Greg Norman was the first tour player to own one.

Hack: a bad swing, or a bad golfer.

Hacking: a series of bad swings.

Halfway house: a snack bar on a golf course.

Hardpan: terrain that's hardpacked and devoid of grass.

Hay: long rough.

Hazard: a bunker or open water area – such as a ditch, lake, river or sea – or anything of similar nature, whether or not it contains water.

Heat: a shot that goes exceptionally long; the ability to hit any club really far. 'He's got heat.'

Helicopter: the throwing motion of a club by a player in which the club twirls through the air like a helicopter blade. Usually done after a bad shot.

Hitting off the deck: to hit a shot off the turf and without a tee; term is usually used in reference to using a driver.

Hole out: hit the ball into the hole.

Homesick gopher: a long putt that goes into the cup.

Honour: the right to hit first off a tee, determined by the lowest score on the previous hole.

Hook: a shot that curves a lot from right to left, for a right-handed player.

Is that any good?: a phrase used after hitting, or watching, a great shot.

Jab: to hit a bad putt.

Jail: a bad position that's probably unplayable, leaving little or no chance to hit a good shot.

Kerplunk: a shot that flies directly into the water.

Kick-in: a super-short putt.

Knife: a 1-iron.

Let the big dog eat: a phrase used to announce that you're going to hit a driver.

Lights out: a very low score ('She shot lights out').

Line drive: a very low shot.

Lip: the edge of the hole on a green; the edge of a bunker.

Lip out: a putt that hits the edge of a hole and changes direction but doesn't go in.

Liquid Draino: a putt that goes straight into the hole, firmly rolling over the front edge of the cup without touching the back edge.

Local rule: a rule that isn't in the *Rules of Golf* but is made up by a tournament committee.

Log cabin: a position deep in the woods.

Long game: shots hit with a full swing that go a long distance.

Long-irons: 1- , 2- and 3-irons.

Looper: a caddie.

Lumberyard: another term for log cabin.

Mark, lift, clean and place: a local rule that tells you what you're allowed to do with your ball in adverse playing conditions. You can mark the ball's location with a tee or coin; lift the ball; clean it; and replace it within a predetermined distance from where the ball originally lay.

Match: a head-to-head competition.

Medallist: the low qualifier in the stroke-play portion of a tournament whose winner is determined by match play.

Mid-irons: the 4- , 5- , 6- and 7-irons.

Mudder: a person who plays well in wet conditions.

Mulligan: an extra try at a shot, usually taken on the first tee; not allowed by the rules but often offered as a courtesy during a friendly game.

Muni: a public course.

Nassau: a gambling term for a three-way bet, including equal wagers on the front nine, the back nine and the overall score.

Net: score for a round, determined by subtracting your handicap from your gross score.

Nineteenth hole: the bar at a golf course, or, at a course with no bar, where you can get a drink after a round.

No-brainer: a shot, usually a putt, that looks too easy too miss.

Nuked it: hit a shot as far as possible.

O.B.: out of bounds.

Obi-Wan Kenobi: a shot that goes out of bounds.

Pelt: a big divot.

Personal scramble: a way of playing alone, whereby the golfer hits as many shots as necessary from each position on the course until he is satisfied with his shot.

Picked-up: another term for ball-in-pocket.

Pill: a golf ball.

Pin: an incorrect but commonly used word for flagstick.

Pipe: a drive down the middle of the fairway. Also used as a verb ('She piped that tee shot').

Played good: the wrong way to say you played well.

Play through: play a hole while the group ahead of you moves to the side to let you pass them.

Plugged: when your ball is embedded in the ground.

Pot bunker: a bunker, usually filled with sand, shaped like a deep pot used for cooking.

Press: a new bet started in the middle of a round, covering a portion or all of the remaining holes. You may only initiate a press if you're losing an existing bet.

Pull: a shot that starts to the left but doesn't curve, for a right-handed player.

Pull-cart: a two- or three-wheeled cart with wheels and a handle, designed to carry your bag.

Pure: description of a perfectly struck shot.

Purse: prize money in a professional tournament.

Push: a shot that starts to the right but doesn't curve, for a right-handed player.

Raked it: played poorly.

Ranger: a person who maintains proper speed of play and safety at a course; another term for marshal.

Relief: a situation in which the rules permit moving your ball with no penalty.

Ringer: a good player disguised as a bad player.

Ripped it: hit the ball solid and far.

Rock: a golf ball; often a very hard ball.

Rough: a cut of grass that is longer than the fairway grass.

Rub of the green: a phrase describing what happens when your ball is accidentally deflected by an outside agency but you can't change the shot's result. (See Rule 19-1 in the *Rules of Golf*.)

Sandbagger: a cheater; usually somebody who plays much better than his handicap.

Scramble: a form of competition in which every player in a group hits, and the group then selects the best shot from which to play their next shot. The team keeps playing until they hole out.

Scrapin' it around: a phrase for not hitting the ball well, but making a good score.

Scratch player: a golfer who competes without using a handicap and usually shoots par. All pros play at scratch.

Seagoer: a holed putt that was very long and undulating.

Set-up: another term for the address position.

Shag bag: a bag for storing used golf balls.

Shank: a shot hit off the hosel of the clubhead that flies on an almost 90 degree line to the right, for a right-handed player.

Shelf: a distinct level on a green.

Short-irons: 8-iron, 9-iron and all wedges.

Short knocker: a short hitter.

Skull: another term for a bladed shot.

Sky ball: a shot that goes very high but not very far.

Slam dunk: a putt that is moving fast when it goes into the hole.

Slashing: another term for hacking.

Slope: one of two gauges measuring the difficulty of a course; the slope is based primarily on length of rough, topography, speed of greens and hazards.

Slow-playing: playing slower than normal to throw off your opponent's rhythm.

Snapper: a low shot that curves sharply from right to left and doesn't go very far, for a right-handed player.

Snap-slice: a shot that curves sharply and fast from left to right, for a right-handed player.

Snowman: a score of eight on a hole; good players sometimes call a round of 80 a 'snowman.'

Spank it: hit the ball with good power.

Spanning your coin: moving a ball marker out of your competitor's line, and then back to its original position after he's putted.

Spun it back: a phrase for a shot that spins back towards the player after landing on the green.

Stadium course: a course designed to accommodate large galleries, with huge turf amphitheatres and mounds surrounding the fairways, greens and tees.

Stick: a good player.

Stick it: a phrase for hitting an approach shot that has almost no roll and stops close to the hole.

Stiff: a description of a shot that stops close to the hole.

Stony: another term for stiff.

The strip: an 18-hole score of 77.

Stripe it: hit it straight.

Stymied: description of your ball when it's stuck behind something, such as a rock or tree.

Sup (*pronounced 'soup'*): a golf course superintendent.

Swale: a distinct low spot with fairly steep sides, on a fairway or a green.

Tall stuff: the tallest rough on a course.

T.C. Chen: a double-hit; when your clubface hits the ball twice on the same stroke. Named after Taiwanese professional T.C. Chen, who lost the 1985 U.S. Open by 1 stroke after double-hitting a chip from thick grass and making a quadruple-bogey 8 on the fifth hole of the final round.

Tee sign: a sign on the tee that shows the par and the yardages from each set of markers on a hole.

Texas wedge: a shot from off the green in which you use a putter.

That plays: a term describing a good shot.

That's gone: what you say when you or a playing partner hits a shot that is flying out of bounds or into trouble.

That's good: what you say when you're conceding a putt to a competitor.

That's history: a shot that's lost or out of bounds.

Tight lie: the position of a ball when it lies on turf, generally hard, with very little grass.

Top: a shot in which you hit the top of the ball.

Tour school: qualifying tournament for a professional tour.

Trap: a commonly used term for a bunker.

Triple: short for triple-bogey (3 over par on a hole).

Trolley: a term for a pull-cart.

Trombones: an 18-hole score of 76.

Twilight: the last few hours of daylight; many public courses offer discounted greens fees in this period.

Up and down: when you take two shots to get into the hole from off the green.

Up and in: another term for up and down.

Vampire lip out: a 180-degree, or more, lip out.

Velcro: when you hit the ball onto the green and it stops exactly where it landed.

Waggle: the small movements you make with the club just before you begin the swing.

Went in the tank: played badly at the end of a round.

Whiff: a swing in which you miss the ball.

Whiskey loop: a series of holes, usually three to five of them, that starts and finishes at the clubhouse.

Worm-burner: a shot that flies very fast and very low.

Yardage marker: a sign on the course indicating the distance to the hole.

Yips: a bad putting problem in which you involuntarily flinch your hands during the stroke.

Zed: another term for jail.

CONCLUSION

Now that you've completed my five-step programme and almost finished this book, what do you think is my most important point? Balance is control? Motion equals power? Play one shot at a time, with no regard for the future or the past? Those concepts are important, but if I leave you with just one piece of advice, I hope it will be this: golf is not about the score.

Golf is a wonderful game, and there's no reason not to have a blast every time you go to the course, whether you shoot 65 or 115. Never let the score make or break your day, and try not to lose sight of what golf really is: whacking a little ball around a huge chunk of grass; and what it's not: trying to take a predetermined number of strokes for a hole.

The second most important point I'd like you to take from my book is this: dream big. Real big. Whatever your goals in golf currently are, quadruple them, and you'll still barely be scratching the surface of what is possible. Tiger Woods and Annika Sorenstam and Karrie Webb have set new standards of excellence on the PGA and LPGA tours, respectively, but by no stretch of the imagination have they – or anybody else in the history of the game – played golf as well as it can be played. That, in fact, is the beauty of golf: everybody can play better. In my lifetime, I fully expect to see a tour pro shoot a round of 55 or below and an aggregate score below 248 for a four-round tournament (that means he or she will average 62 for each round).

Those scores might sound preposterous. But they're not, and the reason is simple: golf has barely tapped the available talent pool. In the United States, less than 10 per cent of the total population plays golf. Imagine what the competition on tour would be like if even half the population in the United States tried hitting a few golf balls. Then imagine if everybody on earth tried the game. In the future, you may hardly hear about pros who today are as good as Annika, Karrie and Tiger, because players of their calibre might be only good, not great, if society takes up golf en masse.

Whatever your goal is in golf, you'll need to balance the time you practise golf with the time you play golf. Great players who I've coached come back to me for help when their games deteriorate, and they often say, 'I've been playing a ton, but I'm shooting a million.'

Indeed, playing golf is fun, but you must practise if you want to play your best. I recommend that you spend at least one-third of your golf time practising. Thus, if you dedicate nine hours a week to golf, you should practise for three of those hours. And when you practise, remember to have fun – play games, create competitions and stretch your imagination to the limit.

Golf is growing, but much slower than you might think. The number of golfers in the United States is inching up, having risen 7.5 per cent from 1996 to 2000 (24.7 million to 26.7 million). The number of children getting into golf is growing much faster, however, having risen 14.3 per cent during the same period. Many of those kids are maturing in the game at a younger age than ever before, and some of them are turning pro. In 2001, Ty Tryon and Kevin Na, a couple of 17-year-olds, turned pro, and Ty made it through Q school and earned a PGA Tour card for 2002. In the women's game over the last few years, a slew of youngsters have been entering the pro ranks before their 20th birthdays, led by Dorothy Delasin and Se Ri Pak, who have both won multiple LPGA tournaments.

Based on the ever-growing youth movement in golf, here is a prediction. By 2020, the oldest players at both the LPGA and the PGA Tour's tournament of champions – season-opening events that include winners from the previous year – won't have reached her and his 30th birthdays.

What does all this mean to you? Whether you're considering becoming a tour professional or you just want to play once a month with your friends, the fact that there's so much room for improvement will, I hope, inspire you to bring a superpositive attitude to the course and dream big.

Wherever you play, you're going to meet a lot of people who think in the past, idolising the records set by players like Nancy Lopez, Byron Nelson and Tiger. But those standards must be kept in perspective. Yes, all those golfers played magnificent golf, but they didn't play perfect golf, so there's a lot of room between their levels of competency and what can be achieved.

My final thought: smile, dream big and keep up with the group in front of you.

ACKNOWLEDGMENTS

If I learned anything during the 18-month process of turning this book from a zany idea into a finished manuscript, it is that there are three things an author must have to be successful.

1. Two cats. My wife and I are blessed to have Max and Nala, a couple of feminine felines who spent many a day (and night) perched by my computer providing affection.
2. A devoted agent. Before embarking on this, my first book, I had believed that agents were overpaid and underworked. Now I know it's the other way around. At least it is with Rob Robertson, whose business and editorial acumen is nonpareil.
3. A spouse who doesn't mind months of neglect. Writing books is a solitary pursuit and not conducive to seeing movies, grocery shopping, doing laundry or parking a car on the streets of New York City. Fortunately, my significant other, Carrie Cohen, became an avid golfer during the last couple of years. So I made an offer a junkie couldn't refuse: a few days of golf lessons with Rudy Duran in exchange for several months of solitary confinement.

Of course, there are many other people who deserve sincere thanks for their inspiration and help with this project. The two who stand out are my grandmother and my mother. Gram got me into golf by giving me lessons when I was four years old. (Tiger and I have *something* in common.) And Mum, who passed away in January 2001, just a few months before Rudy and I completed this book, prodded me to begin caddying when I was 11 years old. I baulked at first, but soon capitulated to her desire to get me on to the links. Now, I am deeply grateful for my ten-year looping career, which provided me with a superb education in golf and life, not to mention a pile of Ben Franklins.

Fore!

Rick Lipsey

I'd first like to thank my mother and father, and my brother and sisters, for their lifelong support.

I would also like to thank Rob Robertson, my agent, and Rick Lipsey, because without them I never would have completed this book. Special thanks, too, to all the staff at golf courses I've worked at. They have helped make my junior programme successful. These people include those in the maintenance crews, in the pro shops, in the coffee shops, and even in the offices.

Of course, I also must thank Earl and Tida Woods for allowing me to help them with their son's development, and Tiger for his support of this book. Also, a big thank you to all the junior golfers who have been such a big part of my golf career. You keep me inspired to improve as a teacher and player.

Rudy Duran